How to
Live a Life
of
Prayer

How to
Live a Life
of
Prayer

Classic Christian Writers on the
Divine Privilege of Prayer

JOHN WESLEY, E. M. BOUNDS,
ANDREW MURRAY, S. D. GORDON

BARBOUR BOOKS
An Imprint of Barbour Publishing, Inc.

© 2018 by Barbour Publishing, Inc.

Compiled and edited by Donna K. Maltese.

Print ISBN 978-1-68322-563-8

eBook Editions:
Adobe Digital Edition (.epub) 978-1-68322-801-1
Kindle and MobiPocket Edition (.prc) 978-1-68322-802-8

Text taken from *How to Pray* by John Wesley, *A 31-Day Guide to Prayer* and *Teach Me to Pray* by Andrew Murray, *Quiet Talks on Prayer* by S. D. Gordon, and *Possibilities in Prayer* by E. M. Bounds, all published by Barbour Publishing, Inc. Some of the text of these writings has been lightly updated for modern readers.

All scripture quotations are taken from the King James Version of the Bible.

This text includes John Wesley's original paraphrases of scripture.

Published by Barbour Books, an imprint of Barbour Publishing, Inc., 1810 Barbour Drive, Uhrichsville, Ohio 44683, www.barbourbooks.com

Our mission is to inspire the world with the life-changing message of the Bible.

Member of the
Evangelical Christian
Publishers Association

Printed in the United States of America.

CONTENTS

Introduction 7
Who 9
    God 9
    Jesus 13
    Holy Spirit 15
    God's Word 17
    You 18
    Others 22
    The Relationship of Prayer Participants 25

What 28
    Prayer 28
    Primacy of Faith 33
    Persistence 36
    Promises 42
    Possibilities 46
    Providence 51
    Power 61
    Limits 66
    Praise and Worship 69
    Presence 74
    Purpose 82
    Petitions 85
    Expectations 89
    Hindrances 94
    Answers 103
    Proof 110

Proof in Bible Days 111
Proof in Present Day 115

When 121

Where 130

Why 137

How (in what way and by what means). 142
    The "How" of God's Will 142
    The "How" of Relationship. 152
    The "How" of Method 156
    The "How" of Approach. 165
    The "How" of Listening 172
    The "How" of Praying for Others. 178

God will answer those who believe in Him and His power when they come to Him, asking, seeking, and knocking with their entire beings. His Son Jesus is the conduit of their voices. His Holy Spirit, the interpreter. Thus, this thing called *prayer* is the believers' vital link and lifeline to the all-powerful Trinity in which they live, move, and have their being.

S. D. Gordon calls prayer "a spirit force," and those who pray "spirit beings." He writes, "prayer is really projecting my spirit, that is, my real personality, to the spot concerned and doing business there with other spirit beings"! E. M. Bounds calls prayer an "energetic force," writing, "Prayer moves men because it moves God to move men. . . . Prayer moves the hand that moves the world."

Then there's John Wesley, who writes about the vitalness of continual prayer: "God's command to 'pray without ceasing' is founded on the necessity we have of his grace to preserve the life of God in the soul, which can no more subsist one moment without it, than the body can without air." Of the life-forming importance of prayer, Andrew Murray writes, "In Jesus' prayer life He manifested two things to us: first, God's Word supplies us with material for prayer and encourages us in expecting everything from God; second, it is only by prayer that we can live such a life so that every word of God can be fulfilled in us."

But how many people know *who* exactly they are praying to or *what* prayer really is? How many know *when* or *where* to pray? How many know *why* they should pray or, even more importantly, *how* to pray?

To help you find your own way into this vital lifeline and hone your current methods, we invite you into *How to Live a Life of Prayer*. This collection of readings by the four classic Christian authors quoted above gives you the means, method, and motive to navigate your way through the who, what, when, where, why, and how of prayer and its power. These authors are: E. M. (Edward McKendree) Bounds (1835–1913), an American preacher, author, and attorney; S. D. (Samuel Dickey) Gordon (1859–1936), an American author, speaker, and lay minister; Andrew Murray (1828–1917), a South African pastor, preacher, author, and missions speaker; and John Wesley (1703–1791), an English preacher, author, and composer.

As you put the knowledge and precepts herein presented into practice with consistency and confidence, our hope is that you will experience the amazing power of prayer in your inner and the outer world. And *our* ongoing prayer is that. . . "the eyes of your understanding being enlightened. . .ye may know what is the hope of [God's] calling, and what [are] the riches of the glory of his inheritance in the saints, and what is the exceeding greatness of his power to us-ward who believe, according to the working of his mighty power" (Ephesians 1:18–19).

Prayer is not a solo endeavor. Several alive and active "beings"—God, Jesus, the Holy Spirit, the Word, you, and others—are involved, each with a particular role to play and special relationship to each other. Although the supernatural participants remain the same, the prayer's prayer is forever changing and evolving in response to the circumstances and growth of the petitioner and those for whom he or she is praying and according to the answers and provisions received. Pray that God would make all this and more clear to you as you consider "who's who" in the cast of prayer participants.

God

A Personal God
E. M. BOUNDS

Prayer ascends to God by an invariable law, even by more than law, by the will, the promise and the presence of a personal God. The answer comes back to earth by all the promise, the truth, the power, and the love of God.

All the Attributes of God
E. M. BOUNDS

God holds all good in His own hands. That good

comes to us through our Lord Jesus Christ because of His all-atoning merits, by asking it in His name. The sole command in which all the others of its class belong is "ask, seek, knock." And the one and sole promise is its counterpart, its necessary equivalent and results: "It shall be given, ye shall find, it shall be opened unto you."

God is so much involved in prayer and its hearing and answering, that all of His attributes and His whole being are centered in that great fact. It distinguishes Him as peculiarly beneficent, wonderfully good, and powerfully attractive in His nature. "O thou that hearest prayer, unto thee shall all flesh come" (Psalm 65:2). . . .

Not only does the Word of God stand surety for the answer to prayer, but all the attributes of God conspire to the same end. God's veracity is at stake in the engagements to answer prayer. His wisdom, His truthfulness, and His goodness are involved. God's infinite and inflexible rectitude is pledged to the great end of answering the prayers of those who call upon Him in time of need. Justice and mercy blend into oneness to secure the answer to prayer. It is significant that the very justice of God comes into play and stands hard by God's faithfulness in the strong promise God makes of the pardon of sins and of cleansing from sin's pollutions in 1 John 1:9: "If we confess our sins, he is faithful and just to forgive us our sins, and to cleanse us from all unrighteousness."

God's kingly relation to man, with all of its authority, unites with the fatherly relation and with all of its tenderness to secure the answer to prayer.

Who God Is
S. D. GORDON

There are five common, everyday words I want to bring you to suggest something of who God is. The first is the word *father*. "Father" stands for loving strength. A father plans, provides for, and protects his loved ones. If you will think of the finest father you ever knew that anybody ever had, think of him now. Then remember this: God is a father, only He is so much finer a father than the finest father you ever knew of. And His will for your life down here is a father's will for the one most dearly loved.

The second word is a finer word, the word *mother*. If father stands for strength, mother stands for love—great, patient, tender, enduring love. What would she not do for her loved one! Think of the finest mother you ever knew, then remember this: God is a mother, only He is so much finer a mother than the finest mother you ever knew.

The references in scripture to God as a mother are numerous. "Under his wings" [Psalm 91:4] is a mother figure. The mother-bird gathers her brood up under her wings [see Matthew 23:37] to feel the heat of her body and for protection. The word *mother* is not used for God in the Bible. I think it is because with God "father" includes "mother." It takes more of the human to tell the story than of the divine. With God, all the strength of the father and all the fine love of the mother are combined in that word *father*. And His will for us is a wise, loving mother's will for the darling of her heart.

The third word is *friend*. I mean a friend who loves you for your sake only and steadfastly loves without regard for any return. If you will think for a moment of the very best friend you ever knew anybody to have, then remember this: God is a friend. Only He is ever so much better a friend than the best friend you ever knew of. And the plan He has thought out for your life is such a one as that word would suggest.

The fourth word I almost hesitate to use. The hesitancy is because the word and its relationship are spoken of lightly. I mean that rare fine word *lover*, where two have met and acquaintance has deepened into friendship, and that in turn into the holiest emotion, the highest friendship. What would he not do for her! She becomes the new human center of his life. In a good sense he worships the ground she walks on. And she will leave wealth for poverty to be with him in the coming days. She will leave home and friends and go to the ends of the earth if his service calls him there. Think of the finest lover, man or woman, you ever knew anybody to have, then remember this—and let me say it in reverent tones—God is a lover. Only He is so much finer a lover than the finest lover you ever knew of. And His will, His plan for your life and mine is a lover's plan for his only loved one.

The fifth word is this fourth word spun a finer degree: *husband*. This is the word on the man side for the most hallowed relationship of earth. This is the lover relationship in its perfection stage. With men *husband* is not always a finer word than lover. The more's the pity. In God's thought a husband is a lover *plus*. He is all that the finest lover is, and more: more tender, more eager, more thoughtful. Two lives are joined and begin living one life. Two wills, yet one. Two persons, yet one purpose. Duality in unity. Call to mind for a moment the best husband you ever knew any woman to have, then remember that God is a husband; only He is an infinitely more thoughtful husband than any you ever knew. And His will for your life is a husband's will for his life's friend and companion.

Now please don't take one of these words and say, "I like that." How we whittle God down to our narrow conceptions! You must take all five words and think the finest meaning into each, and then put them all together to get a close-up idea of God. He is all that, *and more.*

Jesus

Threefold Cord
S. D. GORDON

Jesus came to do somebody's else will. The controlling purpose of His life was to please His Father. That was the secret of the power of His earthly career. Right relationship to God, an intimate prayer-life, marvelous power over men and with men—those are the strands in the threefold cord of His life.

His Divine Business
E. M. BOUNDS

[Jesus Christ's] earthly life was made up largely of hearing and answering prayer. His heavenly life is devoted to the same divine business.

The Rightful Prince
S. D. GORDON

In its simplest meaning, prayer has to do with a conflict. It is the deciding factor in a spirit conflict. The scene of the conflict is the earth. The purpose of the conflict is to decide the control of the earth and its inhabitants. The conflict runs back into the misty ages of the creation time.

The rightful prince of the earth is Jesus, the King's Son. There is a pretender prince who was once rightful prince. He was guilty of a breach of trust. But like King Saul, after his rejection and David's anointing in his place, he has been and is trying his best to hold the realm and oust the rightful ruler.

The rightful Prince is seeking by utterly different means—namely, persuasion—to win the world back to its first allegiance. He had a fierce run-in with the pretender, and after a series of victories won the great victory of the resurrection morning.

There is one peculiarity of this conflict that makes it different from all others: a decided victory and the utter vanquishing of the leading general has not stopped the war. And the reason is remarkable. The Victor has a deep love-ambition to not merely beat the enemy but *win men's hearts, by their free consent.* And so, with marvelous love born of wisdom and courage, the conflict is left open, for men's sake.

Christ as Intercessor
ANDREW MURRAY

He is able also to save them to the uttermost that come unto God by him, seeing he ever liveth to make intercession for them.
HEBREWS 7:25

In His life on earth Christ began His work as Intercessor. Think of the high priestly prayer on behalf of His disciples and of all who would believe in His name through them. Think of His words to Peter, "I have prayed for thee, that thy faith fail not" (Luke 22:32)—a proof of how intensely personal His intercession is. And on the cross He spoke as intercessor: "Father, forgive them" (Luke 23:34).

Now that He is seated at God's right hand, He continues, as our great High Priest, the work of intercession without ceasing. Yet He gives His people power to take part in it. Seven times in His farewell discourse He repeated the assurance that He would do what they asked.

The power of heaven was to be at the disciples' disposal. God waited for the disciples to ask for His grace and power. Through the leading of the Holy Spirit they would know what the will of God was. They would learn in faith to pray in His name. He would present their requests to the Father, and through united intercession the Church would be clothed with the power of the Spirit.

Holy Spirit

One Inlet of Power
S. D. GORDON

There is one inlet of power in the life—the Holy Spirit. He is power. He is in everyone who opens his door to God. He eagerly enters every open door. He comes in by our invitation and consent. His presence within is the vital thing.

But with many of us, while He is inside, He is not in control. He is inside as guest, not as host. He is hindered in His natural movements so that He cannot do what He wants. And so we are not conscious or are only partially conscious of His presence. And others are still less so. But to yield to His mastery, to cultivate His friendship, to give Him full sway—that will result in what is called power.

The Other Christ
E. M. Bounds

How truly does the other Christ, the other Comforter, the Holy Spirit, represent Jesus Christ as the Christ of prayer! This other Christ, the Comforter, plants Himself not in the waste of the mountain nor far into the night, but in the chill and the night of the human heart, to rouse it to the struggle, and to teach it the need and form of prayer. How the divine Comforter, the Spirit of Truth, puts into the human heart the burden of earth's almighty need and makes the human lips give voice to its mute and unutterable groanings!

What a mighty Christ of prayer is the Holy Spirit! How He quenches every flame in the heart but the flame of heavenly desire! How He quiets, like a weaned child, all the self-will, until in will, in brain, and in heart, and by mouth, we pray only as He prays: making "intercession for the saints, according to the will of God" (Romans 8:27).

Master Intercessor
S. D. Gordon

Let the Spirit teach you how to pray. The more you pray, the more you will find yourself saying to yourself, "I don't know how to pray." God understands that and has a plan to cover our need there. There is One who is a master intercessor. He understands praying perfectly. He is the Spirit of prayer. God has sent Him down to live inside you and me, partly to teach us the fine art of prayer. Let Him teach you.

God's Word

Miraculous
E. M. Bounds

Our gospel belongs to the miraculous. It was projected on the miraculous plane. It cannot be maintained but by the supernatural. Take the supernatural out of our holy religion, and its life and power are gone, and it degenerates into a mere mode of morals. The miraculous is divine power. Prayer has in it this same power. Prayer brings this divine power into the ranks of men and puts it to work. Prayer brings into the affairs of earth a supernatural element. Our gospel when truly presented is the power of God. Never was the church more in need of those who can and will test Almighty God. Never did the church need more than now those who can raise up everywhere memorials of God's supernatural power, memorials of answers to prayer, memorials of promises fulfilled.

God in Print
S. D. GORDON

Give the Book of God its place in prayer. Prayer is not talking to God—simply. It is listening first, then talking. Prayer needs three organs of the head: an ear, a tongue, and an eye. First an ear to hear what God says, then a tongue to speak, then an eye to watch for the result. Bible study is the listening side of prayer. The purpose of God comes in through the ear, passes through the heart, taking on the tinge of your personality, and goes out at the tongue as prayer. It is pathetic what a time God has getting a hearing down here. He is ever speaking, but even where there may be some inclination to hear, the sounds of earth are choking out the sound of His voice. God speaks in His Word. The most we know of God comes to us here. This Book is God in print. God Himself speaks in this Book. Studying it keenly, intelligently, reverently will reveal God's great will. What He says will utterly change what you say.

You

Chosen
S. D. GORDON

God will do as a result of the praying of the humblest one here what otherwise He would not do. Yes, I can put it stronger than that, for the Book does. God will do in answer to the prayer of the weakest one here what otherwise He could not do. Listen to Jesus' own words in that last long quiet talk He had with the eleven men between the upper room and the olive grove. "Ye have not chosen me, but I have chosen you, and ordained you, that ye should go and bring forth fruit, and that your fruit should remain: that whatsoever ye shall ask of the Father in my name, he *may* give it you" (John 15:16, emphasis added). Mark that word *may*; not *shall* this time but *may*. "Shall" throws the matter over on God—His purpose. "May" throws it over on us—our cooperation. That is to say, our praying makes it possible for God to do what otherwise He could not do.

One with a True Perspective
S. D. GORDON

The rightly rounded Christian life has two sides: the *out*side and the *inner* side. To most of us the outer side seems the greater. The living, the serving, the giving, the doing, the absorption in life's work, the contact with people—these take the greater thought and time of us all. They seem to be the great business of life even to those of us who thoroughly believe in the inner life.

But when the inner eyes open, the change of perspective is first ludicrous, then terrific, then pathetic. Ludicrous, because of the change of proportions; terrific, because of the issues at stake; pathetic, because of strong men that see not and keep spending their strength whittling sticks. The outer side is narrow in its limits. It has to do with food and clothing, bricks and lumber, time and the passing hour, the culture of the mind, the joys of social contact, the smoothing of the way for the suffering. And it needs not be said that these are right; they belong in the picture; they are its physical background.

The inner side *includes all of these*, and stretches infinitely beyond. Its limits are broad. It touches the inner spirit. It moves in upon the motives, the loves, the heart. It moves out upon the myriad spirit-beings. It moves up to the arm of God in cooperation with His great love-plan for a world.

Shall we follow for a day one who has gotten the true perspective? Here is the outer side: a humble home, checking a ledger, pushing the plow, tending the stock, doing the chores, and all the rest of the end-less, day-by-day, commonplace duties that must be done. This one whom we are following unseen is quietly, cheerfully doing his daily round, with a bit of sunshine in his face, a light in his eye, and lightness in his step, and the commonplace becomes uncommon because of the presence of this man with the uncommon spirit. He is working for God. No, better, he is working with God. He has an unseen Friend at his side. That changes all. The common drudgery ceases to be common and ceases to be drudgery because it is done for such an uncommon Master.

Now here is the inner side where the larger work of life is being done. Here is the quiet bit of time alone with God, with the Book. The door is shut, as the Mas-ter said. Now it is the morning hour with a bit of arti-ficial light, for the sun is busy yet farther east. Now it is the evening hour, with the sun speeding toward west-ern service, and the bed invitingly near. There is a look-ing up into God's face then reverent reading, and then a simple, intelligent pleading with its many variations of this—"Your will be done, in the Victor's name." God Himself is here, in this inner room. The angels are here. This room opens out into and is in direct touch with a spirit space as wide as the earth. The horizon of this room is as broad as the globe. God's presence with this man makes it so.

Today a half hour is spent in China, for its missionaries, its native Christians, its millions. And in through the petitions runs this golden thread— "Victory in Jesus' name today. Your will be done." Tomorrow's bit of time is largely spent in India perhaps. And so this man with the narrow outer horizon and the broad inner horizon pushes his spirit-way around the world. The tide of prayer sweeps quietly, relentlessly day by day.

This is the true Christian life. This man is winning souls and refreshing lives in these far-off lands and in nearby places as truly as though he were in each place. This is the Master's plan. The true follower of Jesus has as broad a horizon as his Master. Jesus thought in continents and seas. His follower prays in continents and seas.

There comes to this man occasional evidences of changes being wrought, yet he knows that these are but the thin line of glory light that speaks of the fuller shining. And with a spirit touched with glad awe that he can help God, a heart full of peace and yearning, and a life fragrant with an unseen Presence he goes steadily on his way.

God's Footing
S. D. GORDON

Prayer is a person giving God a footing on the contested territory of this earth. The person in full touch with God, insistently praying, is God's footing on the enemy's soil. The person wholly given over to God gives

Him a new sub-headquarters on the battlefield from which to work. And the Holy Spirit within that person, on the new spot, will insist on the enemy's retreat in Jesus the Victor's name. That is prayer.

Others

Filled with Love
ANDREW MURRAY

Be ye therefore sober, and watch unto prayer. And above all things have fervent charity among yourselves.
1 PETER 4:7–8

Earnest prayer and fervent love are closely linked. If we pray only for ourselves, we will not find it easy to be in the right attitude toward God. But when our hearts are filled with love for others, we will continue to pray for them, even for those with whom we do not agree.

Prayer holds an important place in the life of love; they are inseparably connected. If you want your love to increase, forget yourself and pray for God's children. If you want to increase in prayerfulness, spend time loving those around you, helping to bear their burdens.

There is a great need for earnest, powerful intercessors! God desires His children to present themselves each day before the throne of grace to pray down the power of the Spirit upon all believers. Unity is strength. Spiritual unity will help us to live unselfishly, wholly for God and others. Let us apply Peter's words to our lives—"earnest in prayer. . .showing deep love for each other."

As we meditate on love to those around us, we will

be drawn into fellowship with God. This will come, not by reading or thinking, but by spending time with the Father and with the Lord Jesus through the Holy Spirit. Love leads to prayer—to believing prayer is given the love of God.

Touching Hearts
S. D. Gordon

Intercession is service: the chief service of a life according to God's plan. It is unlike all other forms of service and superior to them in this: it has fewer limitations. In all other service we are constantly limited by space, bodily strength, equipment, material obstacles, and difficulties involved with differences of personality. Prayer knows no such limitations. It goes directly into men's hearts, quietly passes through walls, and comes into most direct touch with the inner heart and will.

For the Sake of Others
Andrew Murray

The friend took his weary, hungry friend into his house and into his heart, too. He did not excuse himself by saying he had no bread. At midnight he went out to seek food for him. He sacrificed his night's rest and his comfort to find the needed bread. "Charity. . .seeketh not her own" (1 Corinthians 13:4-5). It is the very nature of love to forget itself for the sake of others. It takes their needs and makes them its own. It finds real joy in living and dying for others as Christ did.

The love of a mother for her prodigal son makes her pray for him. When we have true love for others we will have the spirit of intercession.

It is possible to do much faithful and earnest work for others without true love for them. Just as a lawyer or a physician, out of a love of their profession and a high sense of faithfulness to duty, may become deeply involved with the needs of clients or patients without any special love for them, so servants of Christ may give themselves to their work with devotion and self-sacrificing enthusiasm without any strong, Christlike love.

It is this lack of love that causes a lack of prayer. Love will compel us to prayer as that love and diligence are combined with the tender compassion of Christ.

Power in Unity
Andrew Murray

Verily, verily, I say unto you, Whatsoever ye shall ask the Father in my name, he will give it you.
John 16:23

In Jesus' farewell discourse (John 13–17), He presented life in the Spirit in all its power and attractiveness. Through the Holy Spirit God's children can go directly to the Father and ask God to bless the world. Seven times we have the promise repeated: "You can ask for anything in my name, and I will do it" (John 14:13–14; 15:7, 16; 16:23–24, 26). Read these passages over so that you may come to understand how urgently and earnestly our Lord repeated the promise.

During the ten days before Pentecost the disciples proved this. In response to their continuous united prayer, the heavens were opened. The Spirit of God descended to earth, filling them with His life. They received the power of the Spirit that they might impart it to thousands. That power is still the pledge of what

God will do. If God's children will agree with one accord to wait for the promise of the Father each day, there is no limit to what God will do for them.

Christian, remember that the Holy Spirit will dwell in you with divine power, enabling you to testify for Him. But it also means that you may unite with God's children to ask in prayer greater and more wonderful things than the heart can imagine.

The Relationship of Prayer Participants

Oneness of Purpose
S. D. GORDON

The relationship that underlies prayer has an absorbing, controlling purpose: to please Jesus. That sentence may sound simple enough, but there is no sentence I might utter that has a more freshly honed razor-edge to it than that. The purpose that *controls* my action in every matter is this: to please Him. If you have not done so, take it for a day, a week, and use it as a touchstone regarding thought, word, and action. Take it into matters personal, home, business, social, fraternal. It does not mean to ask, "Is this right? Is this wrong?" Not that. There are a great many things that can be proven to not be wrong but that are not best, that are not His preference. . . .

The true basis of prayer is sympathy, oneness of purpose. Prayer is not extracting favors from a reluctant God. It is not passing a check in a bank window for money. That is mandatory. The roots of prayer lie in oneness of purpose. God up yonder, His Victor-Son by His side, and a man down here, in *such sympathetic touch* that God can think His thoughts in this man's mind and have His desires repeated upon the earth as this man's prayer.

The Spirit Glorifies Christ
Andrew Murray

To understand and experience the work of the Holy Spirit you must try to grasp the relationship of the Holy Spirit to the Lord Jesus. Our Lord said that the Spirit would come as a Comforter to the disciples. The Spirit would reveal Him in their hearts. The disciples held onto that promise—they would not miss their Lord but have Him with them always. This made them pray earnestly for the Holy Spirit, for they longed to have Jesus with them always.

This is the meaning of our text—"He shall glorify me: for he shall receive of mine, and shall shew it unto you" (John 16:14). Where there is an earnest desire for the glory of Jesus in the heart of the believer, the Holy Spirit will preserve the presence of Jesus in our hearts. We must not weary ourselves with striving after God's presence. We must quietly endeavor to abide in fellowship with Christ, to love Him and keep His commandments, and to do everything in the name of Jesus. Then we will be able to count upon the secret but powerful working of the Spirit within us.

If our thoughts are always occupied with the Lord Jesus—His love, His joy, His peace—then the Holy Spirit will graciously bring the fruit of the Spirit to ripeness within us.

Carefully Praying the Word

ANDREW MURRAY

And all that heard him [Jesus] were astonished at his understanding and answers.
LUKE 2:47

In Jesus' time on earth He treasured the Word in His heart. In the temptation in the wilderness and on every opportunity that presented itself until His death on the cross, He showed that the Word of God filled His heart.

In Jesus' prayer life He manifested two things to us: first, God's Word supplies us with material for prayer and encourages us in expecting everything from God; second, it is only by prayer that we can live such a life so that every word of God can be fulfilled in us.

How can we come to the place where the Word and prayer may each have its undivided right over us? There is only one answer: Our lives must be wholly transformed.

We must, by faith in what God will do in us, appropriate the heavenly life of Christ as He lived it here on earth. We must have the certain expectation that the Spirit, who filled Jesus with the Word and prayer, will also accomplish that work in us.

Let us understand that God the Holy Spirit is essentially the Spirit of the Word and the Spirit of prayer; He is the Spirit of the Lord Jesus who is in us to make us truly partakers of His life. If we firmly believe this and set our hearts upon it, then there will come a change in our use of God's Word and prayer such as we could not have thought possible.

The "what" of prayer encompasses many things. In this section, after defining prayer itself, our four writers of wisdom address other things, or "whats," that are linked to prayer, such as primacy of faith, persistence, promises, possibilities, providence, power, limits, praise and worship, presence, purpose, petitions, expectations, hindrances, answers, and proof. As you read, ask God to show you "what" He would have you know.

Prayer

Spirit Being, Force, and Personality
S. D. GORDON

Now prayer is a spirit force; it has to do wholly with spirit beings and forces. It is an insistent claiming by a man that the power of Jesus' victory over the great evil-spirit chieftain will extend to particular lives now under his control. The prayer takes on the characteristic of the man praying. He is a spirit being. It becomes a spirit force. It is a projecting into the spirit realm of his spirit personality. Being a spirit force, it has certain qualities or characteristics of disembodied spirit beings. A disembodied spirit being is not limited by space as we embodied folk are. It can go as swiftly as we can think.

Further, spirit beings are not limited by material obstructions such as the walls of buildings. Prayer is really projecting my spirit, that is, my real personality, to the spot concerned and doing business there with other spirit beings. For example, there is a man in a city on the Atlantic seaboard for whom I pray daily. It makes my praying for him tangible and definite to recall that every time I pray my prayer is a spirit force instantly traversing the space between him and me and influencing the spirit beings surrounding him, and so influencing his own will.

Prayer Moves
E. M. Bounds

Prayer is a direct address to God. "In every thing. . .let your requests be made known unto God" (Philippians 4:6). Prayer secures blessings and makes men better because it reaches the ear of God. Prayer is only for the betterment of men when it has affected God and moved Him to do something for men. Prayer affects men by affecting God. Prayer moves men because it moves God to move men. Prayer influences men by influencing God to influence them. Prayer moves the hand that moves the world.

Our Prayer Is God's Opportunity
S. D. Gordon

In its simplest analysis, all prayer must have two parts. First, a God to give, and second, *a man to receive.* Man's willingness is God's channel to the earth. God never crowds or coerces. Everything God does for man and through man He does with man's consent, always. Let it be said that God can do nothing for the man with shut hand and shut life. There must be an open hand

and heart and life *through* which God can give what
He longs to. An open life, an open hand is the pipeline
of communication between the heart of God and this
poor world. Our prayer is God's opportunity to get into
the world that shuts Him out.

An Energetic Force
E. M. BOUNDS

In James 5:13–18. . .we have James' directory for praying:

> *Is any among you afflicted? let him pray. Is any*
> *merry? let him sing psalms. Is any sick among*
> *you? let him call for the elders of the church; and*
> *let them pray over him, anointing him with oil*
> *in the name of the Lord: And the prayer of faith*
> *shall save the sick, and the Lord shall raise him*
> *up; and if he have committed sins, they shall be*
> *forgiven him. Confess your faults one to another,*
> *and pray one for another, that ye may be healed.*
> *The effectual fervent prayer of a righteous man*
> *availeth much. Elias was a man subject to like*
> *passions as we are, and he prayed earnestly that*
> *it might not rain: and it rained not on the earth*
> *by the space of three years and six months. And*
> *he prayed again, and the heaven gave rain, and*
> *the earth brought forth her fruit.*

Here is prayer for one's own needs and intercessory prayer for others; prayer for physical needs and
prayer for spiritual needs; prayer for drought and
prayer for rain; prayer for temporal matters and prayer
for spiritual things. How vast the reach of prayer! How

wonderful under these words its possibilities!

Here is the remedy for affliction and depression of every sort, and here we find the remedy for sickness and for rain in the time of drought. Here is the way to obtain forgiveness of sins. A stroke of prayer paralyzes the energies of nature; stays its clouds, rain, and dew; and blasts field and farm like a dust storm. Prayer brings clouds and rain and fertility to the famished and wasted earth.

The general statement, "The effectual fervent prayer of a righteous man availeth much," is a statement of prayer as an energetic force. Two words are used. One, *effectual*, signifies power in exercise, operative power, while the other, *fervent*, is power as an endowment. Prayer is power and strength, a power and strength which influences God, and is most salutary, widespread, and marvelous in its gracious benefits to man. Prayer influences God. The ability of God to do for man is the measure of the possibility of prayer.

Prayer as Communication
S. D. Gordon

Prayer is the word commonly used for all communication with God. But it should be kept in mind that that word covers and includes three forms of communication. All prayer grows up through and ever continues in three stages.

The first form of prayer is *communion*. That is simply being on good terms with God. It involves the blood of the cross as the basis of our getting and being on good terms. It involves my coming to God through Jesus. It is fellowship with God. Not asking for some particular thing but simply enjoying Him, loving Him, thinking about Him, talking to Him without words. That is the truest worship, thinking how worthy He is of all the best we can possibly bring to Him, and infinitely more. Of necessity it includes confession on my part and forgiveness on God's part, for only with those can we come into the relation of fellowship. Adoration and worship belong to this first phase of prayer.

The second form of prayer is *petition*. And I am using that word now in the narrower meaning of asking something for one's self. Petition is a definite request of God for something I need. A man's whole life is utterly dependent upon the giving hand of God. Everything we need comes from Him. There needs to be a constant stream of petition going up, many times wordless prayer. And there will be a constant return stream of answer and supply coming down. The door between God and one's own self must be kept ever open. The knob to be turned is on our side. He opened His side long ago, propped it open, and threw the knob away. The whole life hinges upon this continual communication with our wondrous God.

The third form of prayer is *intercession*. True prayer never stops with petition for one's self. It reaches out for others. The very word *intercession* implies a reaching out for someone else. It is standing as a go-between, a mutual friend, between God and someone who is either out of touch with Him or is needing special help. Intercession is the climax of prayer. It is the outward drive of prayer. It is the effective end of prayer *outward*. Communion and petition are upward and downward. Intercession rests upon these two as its foundation. Communion and petition store the life with the power of God; intercession lets it out on behalf of others. The first two are necessary for self and ally a man fully with God; this third makes use of that alliance for others. Intercession is the form of prayer that helps God in His great love-plan for winning a planet back to its true sphere.

Primacy of Faith

Faith as a Condition
E. M. BOUNDS

When we consider our Lord's miracles, we discover that quite a number were performed unconditionally. At least there were no conditions accompanying them so far as the divine record shows. At His own instance, without being solicited to do so, in order to glorify God and to manifest His own glory and power, this class of miracles was wrought. Many of His mighty works were performed at the moving of His compassion and at the call of suffering and need, as well as at the call of His power. But a number of them were performed by Him in answer to prayer. Some were wrought in answer to the personal prayers of those who were afflicted. Others were performed in answer to the prayers of the friends of those who were afflicted. Those miracles wrought in answer to prayer are very instructive in the uses of prayer.

In these conditional miracles, faith holds the primacy, and prayer is faith's vicegerent. We have an illustration of the importance of faith as the condition on which the exercise of Christ's power was based, or the channel through which it flowed, in the incident of a visit He made to Nazareth with its results, or rather its lack of results. Here is the record of the case as told in Mark 6:5–6:

And he could there do no mighty work, save that he laid his hands upon a few sick folk, and healed them. And he marvelled because of their unbelief.

Those people at Nazareth may have prayed our Lord to raise their dead, or open the eyes of the blind, or heal the lepers, but it was all in vain. The absence of faith, however much of performance may be seen, restrains the exercise of God's power, paralyzes the arm of Christ, and turns to death all signs of life. Unbelief is the one thing which seriously hinders Almighty God in doing mighty works. Matthew's record of this visit to Nazareth says, "And he did not many mighty works there because of their unbelief" (Matthew 13:58). Lack of faith ties the hands of Almighty God in His working among the children of men. Prayer to Christ must always be based, backed, and impregnated with faith.

The miracle of miracles in the earthly career of our Lord, the raising of Lazarus from the dead, was remarkable for its prayer accompaniment. It was really a prayer issue, something after the issue between the prophets of Baal and Elijah. It was not a prayer for help. It was one of thanksgiving and assured confidence. Let us read it from John 11:41–42:

And Jesus lifted up his eyes, and said, Father, I thank thee that thou hast heard me. And I knew that thou hearest me always: but because of the people which stand by I said it, that they may believe that thou hast sent me.

It was a prayer mainly for the benefit of those who were present, that they might know that God was with Him because He had answered His prayers, and that faith in God might be radiated in their hearts.

Prayer Avails Mightily
E. M. BOUNDS

If we believe God's Word, we are bound to believe that prayer affects God, and affects Him mightily; that prayer avails, and that prayer avails mightily. There are wonders in prayer because there are wonders in God. Prayer has no talismanic influence. It is no mere fetish. It has no so-called powers of magic. It is simply making known our requests to God for things agreeable to His will in the name of Christ. It is just yielding our requests to a Father who knows all things, who has control of all things, and who is able to do all things. Prayer is infinite ignorance trusting to the wisdom of God. Prayer is the voice of need crying out to Him who is inexhaustible in resources. Prayer is helplessness reposing with childlike confidence on the word of its Father in heaven. Prayer is but the verbal expression of the heart of perfect confidence in the infinite wisdom, the power, and the riches of Almighty God, who has placed at our command in prayer everything we need.

Simplicity and Strength
E. M. BOUNDS

What a valuable lesson of faith and intercessory prayer does the miracle of the healing of the centurion's servant bring to us in Matthew 8:5–13! The simplicity and strength of the faith of this Roman officer are remarkable, for he believed that it was not needful for our Lord to go directly to his house in order to have his request granted, "But speak the word only, and my servant shall be healed." And our Lord puts His mark upon this man's faith by saying, "Verily I say unto you, I have not found so great faith, no, not in Israel" (Matthew 8:8, 10). This man's prayer was the expression of his strong faith, and such faith brought the answer promptly.

The same invaluable lesson we get from the prayer miracle of the case of the Syrophenician woman who went to our Lord in behalf of her stricken daughter, making her daughter's case her own, by pleading, "Lord, help me." Here was importunity, holding on, pressing her case, refusing to let go or to be denied. A strong case it was of intercessory prayer and its benefits. Our Lord seemingly held her off for a while but at last yielded and put His seal upon her strong faith: "O woman, great is thy faith: be it unto thee even as thou wilt" (Matthew 15:28). What a lesson on praying for others and its large benefits!

Persistence

A Divine Necessity
ANDREW MURRAY

What things soever ye desire, when ye pray, believe that ye receive them, and ye shall have them.
MARK 11:24

The consequence of sin that makes it impossible for God to give at once is a barrier on God's side as well as ours. The attempt to break through the power of sin is what makes the striving and the conflict of prayer such a reality.

Throughout history people have prayed with a sense that there were difficulties in the heavenly world to overcome. They pleaded with God for the removal of the unknown obstacles. In that persevering supplication they were brought into a state of brokenness, of entire resignation to Him, and of faith. Then the hindrances in themselves and in heaven were both overcome. As God prevails over us, we prevail with God.

God has made us so that the more clearly we see the reasonableness of a demand, the more heartily we will surrender to it. One cause of our neglecting prayer is that there appears to be something arbitrary in the call to such continued prayer. This apparent difficulty is a divine necessity and is the source of unspeakable blessing.

Try to understand how the call to perseverance and the difficulty that it throws in our way is one of our greatest privileges. In the very difficulty and delay will the true blessedness of the heavenly life be found. There we learn how little we delight in fellowship with God and how little we have of living faith in Him. There we learn to trust Him fully and without reservation. There we truly come to know Him.

Step by Step
S. D. GORDON

The enemy yields only what he must. He yields only what is taken, therefore the ground must be taken step by step. Prayer must be definite. He yields only when he must, therefore the prayer must be persistent. He continually renews his attacks, therefore the ground taken must be held against him in the Victor's name. This helps to understand why prayer must be persisted in after we have full assurance of the result, and even after some immediate results have come, or after the general results have started coming.

Watching and Praying
Andrew Murray

Continue in prayer, and watch in the same with thanksgiving; withal praying also for us, that God would open unto us a door of utterance.
Colossians 4:2–3

Do you not see how all depends upon God and prayer? As long as He lives and loves and hears and works, as long as there are souls with hearts closed to the Word, as long as there is work to be done in carrying the Word—pray without ceasing. Continue steadfastly in prayer, watching therein with thanksgiving. These words are for every Christian.

Training in Trust
Andrew Murray

Trouble me not: the door is now shut, and my children are with me in bed; I cannot rise and give thee.
Luke 11:7

The faith of the host in Luke 11 met a sudden and unexpected obstacle—the rich friend refuses to hear: "I cannot rise and give thee." The loving heart had not counted on this disappointment and cannot accept it. The asker presses his threefold plea: Here is my needy friend; you have abundance; I am your friend. Then he refuses to accept a denial. The love that opened his house at midnight and then left it to seek help must conquer.

Here is the central lesson of the parable: in our intercession we may find that there is difficulty and delay in the answer. It may be as if God says, "I can't help you this time." It is not easy to hold fast our confidence that He will hear and then to continue to persevere in full assurance that we shall have what we ask. Even so, this is what God desires from us.

He highly prizes our confidence in Him, which is essentially the highest honor the creature can render the Creator. He will therefore do anything to train us in the exercise of this trust in Him. Blessed the man who is not staggered by God's delay or silence or apparent refusal, but is strong in faith giving glory to God. Such faith perseveres, importunately if need be, and cannot fail to inherit the blessing.

How Are We to Wait?

John Wesley

Seek ye the Lord while he may be found, call ye upon him while he is near.
Isaiah 55:6

Suppose one knows this salvation to be the gift and the work of God, and suppose further that one is convinced also that one does not have this gift, how might one attain to it?

If you say, "Believe, and you will be saved!" they answer, "True, but how shall I believe?" You reply, "Wait upon God."

"Well, but how am I to wait? Using the means of grace, or not? Am I to wait for the grace of God, which brings salvation by using the means of grace, or by laying them aside?"

It cannot be conceived that the Word of God should give no direction in so important a point; or that the Son of God, who came down from heaven for us and for our salvation, should have left us without direction with regard to a question in which our salvation is so nearly concerned. And, in fact, He has *not* left us undirected; He has shown us the way in which we should go. We have only to consult the Word of God. Inquire what is written there. If we simply abide by that, no possible doubt can remain.

According to holy scripture, all who desire the grace of God are to wait for it in the means which He has ordained—*in using, not in laying aside*, prayer; hearing, reading, and meditating on the scriptures; and partaking of the Lord's Supper.

Elements of Persistence
Andrew Murray

What things soever ye desire, when ye pray, believe that ye receive them, and ye shall have them.
Mark 11:24

Persistence has various elements—the main ones are perseverance, determination, and intensity. It begins with the refusal to readily accept denial. This develops into a determination to persevere, to spare no time or trouble, until an answer comes. This grows in intensity until the whole being is given to God in supplication. Boldness comes to lay hold of God's strength. At one time it is quiet; at another, bold. At one point it waits in patience, but at another, it claims at once what it desires. In whatever different shape, persistence always means and knows that God hears prayer; I must be heard.

Think of Abraham as he pleads for Sodom. Time after time he renews his prayer until he has to say, "Oh let not the LORD be angry" (Genesis 18:30). He does not cease until he has learned how far he can go, has entered into God's mind, and has rested in God's will. For his sake Lot was saved. "God remembered Abraham, and sent Lot out of the midst of the overthrow" (Genesis 19:29).

Think of Jacob when he feared to meet Esau. The angel of the Lord met him and wrestled with him. When the angel saw that he did not prevail, he said, "Let me go." Jacob said, "I will not let thee go" (Genesis 32:26). So the angel blessed him there. That boldness pleased God so much that a new name was given to Jacob: Israel, he who strives with God, "for as a prince hast thou power with God and with men, and hast prevailed" (Genesis 32:28).

Persevering Prayer
ANDREW MURRAY

Faith must accept the answer given by God in heaven before it is found on earth. This is the essence of believing prayer. Spiritual things can only be spiritually grasped. The spiritual blessing of God's answer to your prayer must be accepted in your spirit before you see it physically. Faith does this.

A person who not only seeks an answer, but first seeks after the God who gives the answer, receives the power to know that he has obtained what he has asked. If he knows that he has asked according to God's will, he believes that he has received.

There is nothing so heart-searching as this faith, "when ye pray, believe that ye receive them, and ye shall have them" [Mark 11:24]. As we strive to believe, and find we cannot, we are compelled to discover what hinders us. Blessed are those who, with their eyes on God alone, refuse to rest till they have believed what our Lord bids. Here is the place where faith prevails, and prevailing prayer is born out of human weakness. Here enters the real need for persevering prayer that will not rest or go away or give up till it knows it is heard and believes that it has received.

Promises

Promise and Prayer—Inextricably Linked
E. M. Bounds

Without the promise, prayer is eccentric and baseless. Without prayer, the promise is dim, voiceless, shadowy, and impersonal. The promise makes prayer dauntless and irresistible. The apostle Peter declares that God has given to us "exceeding great and precious promises" (2 Peter 1:4). "Precious" and "exceeding great" promises they are, and for this very cause we are to "add to our faith," and supply virtue. It is the addition which makes the promises current and beneficial to us. It is prayer which makes the promises weighty, precious, and practical. The apostle Paul did not hesitate to declare that God's grace so richly promised was made operative and efficient by prayer. "Ye also helping together by prayer for us" (2 Corinthians 1:11). . . .

Prayer makes the promise rich, fruitful, and a conscious reality.

Prayer as a spiritual energy, and illustrated in its enlarged and mighty working, makes way for and brings into practical realization the promises of God. . . .

Prayer takes hold of the promise and conducts it to its marvelous ends, removes the obstacles, and makes a highway for the promise to its glorious fulfillment.

While God's promises are "exceeding great and precious," they are specific, clear, and personal. [See God's promise to Abraham in Genesis 22:15–18.]

Author and Perfecter of Our Faith
ANDREW MURRAY

"I believe, help thou mine unbelief."
MARK 9:24

What a treasure of encouragement these words from Mark contain. Jesus had said to the father who had asked Him to heal his child: "Anything is possible if a person believes" (Mark 9:23 paraphrased). The father felt that Christ was throwing the responsibility on him. If he believed, the child could be healed. But he felt his faith was totally inadequate. Yet as he looked in the face of Christ, he felt assured that the love which was willing to heal would also be ready to help him with his weak faith. So he cried: "I do believe, but help me not to doubt." Christ heard the prayer, and the child was healed.

Christ will always accept the faith that puts its trust in Him. Remember the mustard seed. If it is put into the ground and allowed to grow, it becomes a great tree. The weakest faith is made strong and bold when it trusts Christ—the Author and Perfecter of our faith.

Take the hidden seed of little faith and plant it in your heart. Rest on God's promise as you bring it to Him in prayer. He will certainly embrace the trembling faith that clings to Him and will not let Him go. A weak faith in an almighty Christ will become the great faith that can remove mountains.

The Solid Ground
E. M. BOUNDS

Prayer in its usual uniform and deep current is conscious conformity to God's will, based upon the direct promise of God's Word, and under the illumination and application of the Holy Spirit. Nothing is surer than that the Word of God is the sure foundation of prayer. We pray just as we believe God's Word. Prayer is based directly and specifically upon God's revealed promises in Christ Jesus. It has no other ground upon which to base its plea. All else is shadowy, sandy, fickle. Not our feelings, not our merits, not our works, but God's promise is the basis of faith and the solid ground of prayer.

Personal
E. M. BOUNDS

Let it be noted that God's promises are always personal and specific. They are not general, indefinite, or vague. They do not have to do with multitudes and classes of people in a mass, but are directed to individuals. They deal with persons. Each believer can claim the promise as his own. God deals with each one personally, so that every saint can put the promises to the test. "Prove me now herewith, saith the LORD" (Malachi 3:10). No need of generalizing nor of being lost in vagueness. The praying saint has the right to put his hand upon the promise and claim it as his own, one made especially to him, and one intended to embrace all his needs, present and future.

With the Intercession of the Holy Spirit
ANDREW MURRAY

We know not what we should pray for as we ought: but the Spirit itself maketh intercession for us with groanings which cannot be uttered.
ROMANS 8:26

In your ignorance and feebleness believe in the secret indwelling and intercession of the Holy Spirit within you. Yield yourself to His life and leading habitually. He will help your infirmities in prayer. Plead the promises of God even where you do not see how they are to be fulfilled. God knows the mind of the Spirit, because He maketh intercession for the saints according to the will of God. Pray with the simplicity of a little child; pray with the holy awe and reverence of one in whom God's Spirit dwells and prays.

Hand in Hand
E. M. BOUNDS

The promise of the Holy Spirit to the disciples in Luke 24:49 was in a very marked way the "promise of my Father," but it was only realized after many days of continued and importunate praying. The promise was clear and definite that the disciples should be endued with power from on high, but as a condition of receiving that power of the Holy Spirit, they were instructed to "tarry. . .in the city of Jerusalem, until ye be endued with power from on high." The fulfillment of the promise depended upon the "tarrying." The promise of this "enduement of power" was made sure by prayer. Prayer sealed it to glorious results. So we find it written in Acts 1:14, "These all continued with one accord in prayer and supplication, with the women." And it is significant that it was while they were praying, resting their expectations on the surety of the promise, that the Holy Spirit fell upon them and they were all "filled with the Holy Ghost" (Acts 2:4). The promise and the prayer went hand in hand.

Prayer Obtains and Creates Promises
E. M. Bounds

Prayer in its legitimate possibilities goes out on God Himself. Prayer goes out with faith not only in the promise of God, but faith in God Himself, and in God's ability to do. Prayer goes out not on the promise merely, but "obtains promises," and creates promises.

Elijah had the promise that God would send the rain, but no promise that He would send the fire. But by faith and prayer, he obtained the fire as well as the rain, but the fire came first.

Possibilities

Vast Possibilities
E. M. Bounds

How vast are the possibilities of prayer! How wide is

its reach! What great things are accomplished by this divinely appointed means of grace! It lays its hand on Almighty God and moves Him to do what He would not otherwise do if prayer was not offered. It brings things to pass which would never otherwise occur. The story of prayer is the story of great achievements. Prayer is a wonderful power placed by Almighty God in the hands of His saints, which may be used to accomplish great purposes and to achieve unusual results. Prayer reaches to everything, takes in all things great and small which are promised by God to the children of men. The only limits to prayer are the promises of God and His ability to fulfill those promises. "Open thy mouth wide, and I will fill it" (Psalm 81:10).

The Possibilities of Prayer and Faith
E. M. Bounds

The possibilities of prayer are the possibilities of faith. Prayer and faith are Siamese twins. One heart animates them both. Faith is always praying. Prayer is always believing. Faith must have a tongue by which it can speak. Prayer is the tongue of faith. Faith must receive. Prayer is the hand of faith stretched out to receive. Prayer must rise and soar. Faith must give prayer the wings to fly and soar. Prayer must have an audience with God. Faith opens the door, and access and audience are given. Prayer asks. Faith lays its hand on the thing asked for.

God's Rectitude and Power
E. M. Bounds

Pure praying remedies all ills, cures all diseases, relieves all situations, however dire, most calamitous, most fearful and despairing. Prayer to God, pure praying, relieves dire situations because God can relieve when no one else can. Nothing is too hard for God. No cause is hopeless which God undertakes. No case is mortal when Almighty God is the physician. No conditions are despairing which can deter or defy God. . . .

No hopeless conditions, no accumulation of difficulties, and no desperation in distance or circumstance can hinder the success of real prayer. The possibilities of prayer are linked to the infinite rectitude and to the omnipotent power of God. There is nothing too hard for God to do. God has pledged that if we ask, we shall receive. God can withhold nothing from faith and prayer.

The Striking Illustration of Samuel
E. M. Bounds

Samuel, under the judges of Israel, fully illustrates the possibility and the necessity of prayer. He himself was the beneficiary of the greatness of faith and prayer in a mother who knew what praying meant. Hannah, his mother, was a woman of mark, in character and in piety, who was childless. That privation was a source of worry and weakness and grief. She sought unto God for relief, and prayed and poured out her soul before the Lord. She continued her praying, in fact she multiplied her praying, to such an extent that to old Eli she seemed to be intoxicated, almost beside herself in the intensity of her supplications. She was specific in her prayers. She wanted a child. For a man child she prayed.

And God was specific in His answer. A man child

God gave her, a man indeed he became. He was the creation of prayer and grew himself to a man of prayer. He was a mighty intercessor, especially in emergencies in the history of God's people. The epitome of his life and character is found in the statement, "Samuel cried unto the LORD for Israel; and the LORD heard him" (1 Samuel 7:9). The victory was complete, and the Ebenezer was the memorial of the possibilities and necessity of prayer.

Again, at another time, Samuel called unto the Lord, and thunder and rain came out of season in wheat harvest. Here are some statements concerning this mighty intercessor, who knew how to pray, and whom God always regarded when he prayed: "Samuel. . .cried unto the LORD all night" (1 Samuel 15:11).

Says he at another time in speaking to the Lord's people, "Moreover as for me, God forbid that I should sin against the LORD in ceasing to pray for you" (1 Samuel 12:23). These great occasions show how this notable ruler of Israel made prayer a habit, and that this was a notable and conspicuous characteristic of his dispensation. Prayer was no strange exercise to Samuel. He was accustomed to it. He was in the habit of praying, knew the way to God, and received answers from God. Through him and his praying God's cause was brought out of its low, depressed condition, and a great national revival began, of which David was one of its fruits.

Samuel was one of the notable men of the old dispensation who stood out prominently as one who had great influence with God in prayer. God could not deny anything he asked of Him. Samuel's praying always affected God and moved God to do what would not have otherwise been done had he not prayed. Samuel stands out as a striking illustration of the possibilities of prayer. He shows conclusively the achievements of prayer.

The Measure of God's Ability
E. M. Bounds

Nothing is too hard for the Lord to do. As Paul declared, He "is able to do exceeding abundantly above all that we ask or think" (Ephesians 3:20). Prayer has to do with God, with His ability to do. The possibility of prayer is the measure of God's ability to do.

The "all things," the "all things whatsoever," and the "anything," are all covered by the ability of God. The urgent entreaty reads, "Whatsoever ye shall ask in prayer" (Matthew 21:22), because God is able to do anything and all things that my desires may crave and that He has promised. In God's ability to do, He goes far beyond man's ability to ask. Human thoughts, human words, human imaginations, human desires, and human needs cannot in any way measure God's ability to do.

Illimitable
E. M. Bounds

Paul in his remarkable prayer in Ephesians, chapter three, honors the illimitable possibilities of prayer and glorifies the ability of God to answer prayer. Closing that memorable prayer, so far-reaching in its petitions, and setting forth the very deepest religious experience, he declares that God "is able to do exceeding abundantly above all that we ask or think." He makes prayer all-inclusive, comprehending all things, great and small. There is no time nor place which prayer does not cover and sanctify. All things in earth and in heaven, everything for time and for eternity, all are embraced in prayer. Nothing is too great and nothing is too small to be the subject of prayer.

Providence

The Trinity of Prayer, Providence, and the Holy Spirit
E. M. BOUNDS

Prayer and the divine providence are closely related. They stand in close companionship. They cannot possibly be separated. So closely connected are they that to deny one is to abolish the other. Prayer supposes a providence, while providence is the result of and belongs to prayer. All answers to prayer are but the intervention of the providence of God in the affairs of men. Providence has to do specially with praying people. Prayer, providence, and the Holy Spirit are a trinity, which cooperate with each other and are in perfect harmony with one another. Prayer is but the request of man for God through the Holy Spirit to interfere in behalf of him who prays. . . .

What is called "divine providence" is simply Almighty God governing the world for its best interests and overseeing everything for the good of mankind. . . .

God's hand is in everything. None are beyond Him

nor beneath His notice. Not that God orders every-thing which comes to pass. Man is still a free agent, but the wisdom of Almighty God comes out when we remember that while man is free and the devil is abroad in the land, God can superintend and overrule earth's affairs for the good of man and for His glory and cause even the wrath of man to praise Him.

Nothing occurs by accident under the superinten-dence of an all-wise and perfectly just God. Nothing happens by chance in God's moral or natural govern-ment. God is a God of order, a God of law, but none the less a superintendent in the interest of His intel-ligent and redeemed creatures. Nothing can take place without the knowledge of God. . . .

Jesus Christ set this matter at rest when He said in Matthew 10:29–31:

Are not two sparrows sold for a farthing? and one of them shall not fall on the ground without your Father. But the very hairs of your head are all numbered. Fear ye not there-fore, ye are of more value than many sparrows.

God cannot be ruled out of the world. The doctrine of prayer brings Him directly into the world and moves Him to a direct interference with all of this world's affairs.

Divine Overseer
E. M. BOUNDS

"The angel of the LORD encampeth round about them that fear him, and delivereth them" (Psalm 34:7). And nothing can touch those who fear God only with the permission of the angel of the Lord. Nothing can break through the encampment without the permission of the captain of the Lord's hosts. Sorrows, afflictions, want, trouble, or even death, cannot enter this divine encampment without the consent of Almighty God, and even then it is to be used by God in His plans for the good of His saints and for carrying out His plans and purposes:

For I am persuaded, that neither death, nor life, nor angels, nor principalities, nor powers, nor things present, nor things to come, nor height, nor depth, nor any other creature, shall be able to separate us from the love of God, which is in Christ Jesus our Lord. (Romans 8:38–39)

These evil things, unpleasant and afflictive, may come with divine permission, but God is on the spot, His hand is in all of them, and He sees to it that they are woven into His plans. He causes them to be over-ruled for the good of His people, and eternal good is brought out of them. These things, with hundreds of others, belong to the disciplinary processes of Almighty God in administering His government for the children of men.

The providence of God reaches as far as the realm of prayer. It has to do with everything for which we pray. Nothing is too small for the eye of God, nothing too insignificant for His notice and His care. God's providence has to do with even the stumbling of the feet of His saints. Psalm 91:11–12 reads:

For he shall give his angels charge over thee, to keep thee in all thy ways. They shall bear thee up in their hands, lest thou

Read again our Lord's words about the sparrow, for He says in Luke 12:6, "Are not five sparrows sold for two farthings, and not one of them is forgotten before God?" Paul asks the pointed question, "Doth God take care for oxen?" (1 Corinthians 9:9). His care reaches to the smallest things and has to do with the most insignificant matters which concern men. He who believes in the God of providence is prepared to see His hand in all things which come to him and can pray over everything.

Not that the saint who trusts the God of providence, and who takes all things to God in prayer, can explain the mysteries of divine providence, but the praying ones recognize God in everything, see Him in all that comes to them, and are ready to say as John said to Peter at the Sea of Galilee, "It is the Lord" (John 21:7).

Praying saints do not presume to interpret God's dealings with them nor undertake to explain God's providences, but they have learned to trust God in the dark as well as in the light, to have faith in God even when "cares like a wild deluge come, and storms of sorrow fall."

Job declared: "Though he slay me, yet will I trust in him" (Job 13:15). Praying saints rest themselves upon the words of Jesus to Peter, "What I do thou knowest not now, but thou shalt know hereafter" (John 13:7). None but the praying ones can see God's hands in the providences of life. "Blessed are the pure in heart: for they shall see God" (Matthew 5:8)—shall see God here in his providences, in His Word, in His church. These are they who do not rule God out of earth's affairs and who believe God interferes with matters of earth for them.

Prayer brings God's providence into action. Prayer puts God to work in overseeing and directing earth's affairs for the good of men. Prayer opens the way when it is shut up or straitened.

Providence deals more especially with temporalities. It is in this realm that the providence of God shines brightest and is most apparent. It has to do with food and raiment, with business difficulties, with strangely interposing and saving from danger, and with helping in emergencies at very opportune and critical times.

The feeding of the Israelites during the wilderness journey is a striking illustration of the providence of God in taking care of the temporal wants of His people. His dealings with those people show how He provided for them in that long pilgrimage.

Our Lord teaches this same lesson of a providence which clothes and feeds His people, in the Sermon on the Mount, when He says in Matthew 6:25, "Take no thought for your life, what ye shall eat, or what ye shall drink; nor yet for your body, what ye shall put on." Then He directs attention to the fact that it is God's providence which feeds the fowls of the air, clothes the lilies of the field, and asks if God does all this for birds and flowers, will He not care for them?

All of this teaching leads up to the need of a childlike, implicit trust in an overruling providence, which looks after the temporal wants of the children of men. And let it be noted specially that all this teaching stands closely connected in the utterances of our Lord with what He says about prayer, thus closely connecting a divine oversight with prayer and its promises.

Providence Leading to Salvation

JOHN WESLEY

The statutes of the LORD are right, rejoicing the heart.
PSALM 19:8

There is a kind of order wherein God Himself is generally pleased to use these means in bringing a sinner to salvation. One goes senselessly on in his own way. God comes upon him unaware—by an awakening sermon or conversation, an awful providence, or a stroke of His convincing Spirit without any outward means. Having now a desire to flee from the wrath of God, he purposely goes to hear how it may be done. If he finds a preacher who speaks to the heart, he is amazed and begins searching the scriptures.

The more he *hears* and *reads*, the more convinced he is; the more he meditates day and night. By these means, the arrows of conviction sink deeper into his soul. He begins to *talk* of the things of God and to *pray* to Him, scarce knowing what to say. Perhaps it is only in "groans which cannot be uttered," perhaps doubting whether the high and lofty God will regard such a sinner as he. So he goes to pray with those who know God, in the congregation. He observes others partaking of the Lord's Supper. He thinks, "Christ has said, 'Do this!' How is it that I do not? I am too great a sinner; I am not worthy."

He struggles awhile, finally breaking through; and so he continues in God's way: *in hearing, reading, meditating, praying, and partaking of the Lord's Supper*; till, in the manner that pleases Him, God speaks, "Your faith has saved you. Go in peace."

Two Kinds of Providences

E. M. Bounds

Two kinds of providences are seen in God's dealings with men: direct providences and permissive providences. God orders some things; others He permits. But when He permits an afflictive dispensation to come into the life of His saint, even though it originate in a wicked mind and it be the act of a sinner, yet before it strikes His saint and touches him, it becomes God's providence to the saint. In other words, God consents to some things in this world, without in the least being responsible for them, or in the least excusing him who originates them. Many of them are very painful and afflictive, but such events or things always become to the saint of God the providence of God to him. So that the saint can say in each and all of these sad and distressing experiences, "It is the LORD; let him do what seemeth him good" (1 Samuel 3:18). Or with the psalmist, he may say, "I was dumb; I opened not my mouth, because thou didst it" (Psalm 39:9).

This was the explanation of all of Job's severe afflictions. They came to him in the providence of God, even though they had their origin in the mind of Satan, who devised them and put them into execution. God gave Satan permission to afflict Job, to take away his property, and to rob him of his children. But Job did not attribute these things to blind chance, nor to accident, neither did he charge them to satanic agency, but said, "The LORD gave, and the LORD hath taken away; blessed be the name of the LORD" (Job 1:21). He took these things as coming from his God, whom he feared and served and trusted.

And to the same effect are Job's words to his wife when she left God out of the question and wickedly told her husband, "Curse God, and die." Job replied, "Thou speakest as one of the foolish women speaketh. What? shall we receive good at the hand of God, and shall we not receive evil?" (Job 2:9–10).

It is no surprise under such a view of God's dealings with Job that it should be recorded there of this man of faith, "In all this did not Job sin with his lips," and in another place was it said, "In all this Job sinned not, nor charged God foolishly" (Job 1:22). In nothing concerning God and the events of life do men talk more foolishly and even wickedly than in ignorantly making up their judgments on the providences of God in this world. Oh that we had men after the type of Job, who though afflictions and privations are severe in the extreme, yet they see the hand of God in providence and openly recognize God in it.

The sequel to all these painful experiences are but illustrations of that familiar text of Paul in Romans 8:28, "And we know that all things work together for good to them that love God." Job received more in the end than was ever taken away from him. He emerged from under these tremendous troubles with victory and became till this day the exponent and example of great patience and strong faith in God's providences. "Ye have heard of the patience of Job" (James 5:11), rings down the line of divine revelation. God took hold of the evil acts of Satan, worked them into His plans, and brought great good out of them. He made evil work out for good without in the least endorsing the evil or conniving at it.

We have the same gracious truth of divine

providence evidenced in the story of Joseph and his brethren, who sold him wickedly into Egypt and forsook him and deceived their old father. All this had its origin in their evil minds. And yet when it reached God's plans and purposes, it became God's providence both to Joseph and to the future of Jacob's descendants. Hear Joseph in Genesis 45:5–8, as he spoke to his brethren after he had discovered himself to them down in Egypt—in which he traces all the painful events back to the mind of God and made them have to do with fulfilling God's purposes concerning Jacob and his posterity:

Now therefore be not grieved, nor angry with yourselves, that ye sold me hither: for God did send me before you to preserve life. . . . And God sent me before you to preserve you a posterity in the earth, and to save your lives by a great deliverance. So now it was not you that sent me hither, but God.

. . . Things which come to us from second causes are no surprise to God, nor are they beyond His control. His hand can take hold of them in answer to prayer, and He can make afflictions, from whatever quarter they may come, work for us "a far more exceeding and eternal weight of glory" (2 Corinthians 4:17).

Recognizing Providence
E. M. Bounds

The providence of God goes before His saints, opens the way, removes difficulties, solves problems, and brings deliverances when escape seems hopeless. God brought Israel out of Egypt by the hand of Moses, his chosen leader of that people. They came to the Red Sea, but there were the waters in front, with no crossing nor bridges. On one side were high mountains and behind came the hosts of Pharaoh. Every avenue of escape was closed. There seemed no hope. Despair almost reigned. But there was one way open which men overlooked, and that was the upward way. A man of prayer, Moses, the man of faith in God, was on the ground. This man of prayer, who recognized God in providence, with commanding force, spoke to the people on this wise in Exodus 14:13: "Fear ye not, stand still, and see the salvation of the LORD."

With this he lifted up his rod, and, according to divine command, he stretched his hand over the sea. The waters divided, and the command issued forth, "Speak unto the children of Israel that they go forward." And Israel went over the sea dry shod. God had opened a way, and what seemed an impossible emergency was remarkably turned into a wonderful deliverance. Nor is this the only time that God has interposed in behalf of His people when their way was shut up.

The Story of Prayer and Providence
E. M. Bounds

The Old Testament especially, but also the New Testament, is the story of prayer and providence. It is the tale of God's dealings with men of prayer, men of faith in His direct interference in earth's affairs, and with God's manner of superintending the world in the interest of His people and in carrying forward His work in His plans and purposes in creation and redemption.

Divine Power Working within
ANDREW MURRAY

Finally. . .be strong in the Lord, and in the power of his might.
EPHESIANS 6:10

Since we as Christians have no strength of our own, where may we get it? Notice the answer: Be strong with the Lord's mighty power.

Paul had spoken of this power in the earlier part of Ephesians (1:17–20). He had prayed to God to give them the Spirit that they might know the greatness of His power which He displayed when He raised Christ from the dead. This is the literal truth: the greatness of His power which raised Christ from the dead works in every believer. We hardly believe it and much less experience it. That is why Paul prays that God would teach us to believe in His almighty power.

In Ephesians 3:16–17, Paul asks the Father to strengthen them by His Spirit, that Christ might dwell in their hearts. And then in verses 20–21: "Now unto him that is able to do exceeding abundantly above all that we ask or think, according to the power that worketh in us, unto him be glory."

Read over these Scriptures again and pray for God's Spirit to make these words real to you. Believe in the divine power working in you. Pray that the Holy Spirit may reveal it to you. Appropriate the promise that God will show His power in your heart, supplying all your needs. It is clear that much time is needed with the Father and the Son, if you would experience the power of God within you.

Commanding the Powers of Heaven
ANDREW MURRAY

I have set watchmen upon thy walls, O Jerusalem, which shall never hold their peace day nor night: ye that make mention of the LORD, keep not silence.
ISAIAH 62:6

And he said unto them, Which of you shall have a friend, and shall go unto him at midnight, and say unto him, Friend, lend me three loaves; for a friend of mine in his journey is come to me, and I have nothing to set before him? And he from within shall answer and say, Trouble me not: the door is now shut, and my children are with me in bed; I cannot rise and give thee. I say unto you, though he will not rise and give him, because he is his friend, yet because of his importunity he will rise and give him as many as he needeth.
LUKE 11:5–8

Prayer is the one power on earth that commands the power of heaven. The early days of the Church are a great object lesson of what prayer can do. Prayer can pull down the treasures of heaven into earth.

Prayer is both indispensable and irresistible. Unknown blessing is stored up for us in heaven; that power will make us a blessing to men and enable us to do any work or face any danger. It is the one secret of success. It can defy all the power of the world and prepare men to conquer that world for Christ.

Prayer Power in the Vine

Andrew Murray

Our power in prayer depends upon our life. When our life is right, we will know how to pray in a way pleasing to God, and our prayer will be answered. "If ye abide in me, and my words abide in you, ye shall ask what ye will, and it shall be done unto you" (John 15:7). According to James it is the prayer of a righteous man that "availeth much" (James 5:16).

In the parable of the vine Jesus taught that the healthy, vigorous Christian may ask what he or she wishes and will receive it. He says, "If you stay joined to me and my words remain in you, you may ask any request you like, and it will be granted." Again He says, "Ye have not chosen me, but I have chosen you, and ordained you, that ye should go and bring forth fruit, and that your fruit should remain: that whatsoever ye shall ask of the Father in my name, he may give it you" (John 15:16).

What life must one lead to bear fruit? What must a person be in order to pray with results? What must one do to receive what he or she asks? The answer is simple. Live as a branch depending on the vine for strength. The source of power in prayer is the vine. If we are branches, abiding in Christ, the vine, He will supply the power. If we trust the vine, then we can ask what we wish and it will be granted.

The Power of Assurance

Andrew Murray

If ye abide in me, and my words abide in you, ye shall ask what ye will, and it shall be done unto you.
JOHN 15:7

Before Jesus went to heaven, He taught His disciples two great lessons in regard to their relationship to Him in the work they had to do.

The one was that, in heaven, Jesus would have much more power than He had here on earth. He would now use that power through His disciples for the salvation of men.

The other was that without Him they could do nothing. Their first and chief work would therefore be to bring everything they wanted done to Him in prayer. In His farewell discourse, Jesus repeats the promise seven times: "Remain in me, pray in my name." "Ask any request you like and it will be granted." You can count on it!

With these truths written in their hearts, He sent the disciples out into the world to accomplish His work. The disciples on earth always looked up to Him in prayer, fully confident that He would hear their prayer. The first and only condition is an unflinching confidence in the power of His promise.

The same condition applies for us today. Close, abiding fellowship with Christ begins with deep dependence and unceasing prayer. It is only then that we can do our work in the full assurance that God has heard our prayer and will be our source of strength.

Resurrection Power
Andrew Murray

[I] cease not to give thanks for you, making mention of you in my prayers; that the God of our Lord Jesus Christ. . .may give unto you the spirit of wisdom. . .that ye may know. . . the exceeding greatness of his power to us-ward who believe.
Ephesians 1:16–19

This is one of the great texts that will make our faith strong and bold. Paul was writing to believers who had been sealed with the Holy Spirit. Yet he felt the need to pray for them for the enlightening of the Holy Spirit. They needed to know that it was the mighty power of God that was working in them. It was the very same power by which God raised Christ from the dead.

When Christ died on the cross, He died under the weight of the sin of the world and its curse. When He descended into the grave, it was under the weight of all that sin that He was buried. The power of death had apparently conquered Him. But the mighty power of God raised Christ from the dead to a place of honor at God's right hand.

It is that very same power that is working in us every day of our lives. The God Who said to Abraham, "Is any thing too hard for the LORD?" (Genesis 18:14), pledges to work His power in us, too, if we will learn to trust Him.

Pray in faith to God and trust His Holy Spirit to enable us to claim nothing less than the exceeding greatness of this Resurrection power working in us.

The Church's Praying Power
ANDREW MURRAY

When we pray consistently we will receive an entrance into God's will of which we would otherwise know nothing. We will receive blessing above all we ask or think. The teaching and power of the Holy Spirit are unalterably linked to prayer.

The power that the Church's prayer has is shown

not only as the apostles pray but also as the Christian community does. In Acts 12 Peter is in prison awaiting execution. The death of James had aroused the Church to a sense of great danger; the thought of losing Peter, too, wakened all their energies. They went to prayer.

Prayer was effective; Peter was delivered. When he came to the house of Mary he found "many were gathered together praying" (Acts 12:12). Double chains, soldiers, and the iron gate—all gave way before the power from heaven that prayer brought to his rescue. The power of the Roman Empire was nothing in the presence of the power that the Church wielded in prayer.

Those Christians stood in close and living relationship with their Lord. They knew well that the words "I have been given complete authority" and "Be sure of this: I am with you always" were absolutely true. They had faith in His promise to hear them whatever they asked. They prayed in the assurance that the powers of heaven not only could work on earth but also that they would work at the Church's request on its behalf.

Limits

Neglect of Prayer
E. M. Bounds

Alas! how the unbelief of men has limited the power of God to work through prayer! What limitations have disciples of Jesus Christ put upon prayer by their prayerlessness! How the church, with her neglect of prayer, has hedged about the gospel and shut up doors of access!

Unbelief of God's Concern
E. M. Bounds

Unbelief in the doctrine that prayer covers all things which have to do with the body and business affairs breeds undue anxiety about earth's affairs, causes unnecessary worry, and creates very unhappy states of mind. How much needless care would we save ourselves if we but believed in prayer as the means of relieving those cares and would learn the happy art of casting all our cares in prayer upon God, "who careth for us"! Unbelief in God as One who is concerned about even the smallest affairs which affect our happiness and comfort limits the Holy One of Israel, and makes our lives altogether devoid of real happiness and sweet contentment.

Unfaith
E. M. Bounds

The only condition which restrains God's power, and which disables Him to act, is unfaith. He is not limited in action nor restrained by the conditions which limit men.

Ignoring Promises
E. M. Bounds

We tread altogether too gingerly upon the great and precious promises of God, and too often we ignore them wholly. The promise is the ground on which faith stands in asking of God. This is the one basis of prayer. We limit God's ability. We measure God's ability and willingness to answer by prayer by the standard of men. We limit the Holy One of Israel. How full of benefaction and remedy to suffering mankind are the promises as given us by James in his epistle, fifth chapter! How personal and mediate do they make God in prayer! They are a direct challenge to our faith. They are encouraging to large expectations in all the requests we make of God. Prayer affects God in a direct manner and has its aim and end in affecting Him. Prayer takes hold of God and induces Him to do large things for us, whether personal or relative, temporal or spiritual, earthly or heavenly.

The Measure of Your Asking
E. M. Bounds

God's only condition and limitation of prayer is found in the character of the one who prays. The measure of our faith and praying is the measure of His giving. As our Lord said to the blind man in Matthew 9:29, "According to your faith be it unto you," so it is the same in praying, "According to the measure of your asking, be it unto you." God measures the answer according to the prayer. He is limited by the law of prayer in the measure of the answers He gives to prayer. As is the measure of prayer, so will be the answer.

If the person praying has the characteristics which warrant praying, then the possibilities are illimitable. They are declared to be "all things whatsoever." Here is no limitation in character or kind, in circumference or condition. The man who prays can pray for anything and for everything, and God will give everything and anything. If we limit God in the asking, He will be limited in the giving.

Praise and Worship

Continual Reaction
JOHN WESLEY

Watch ye therefore, and pray always, that ye may be accounted worthy to escape all these things that shall come to pass.
LUKE 21:36

The life of God in the soul of the believer immediately and necessarily implies a continual action of God upon the soul by the inspiration of God's Holy Spirit and a reaction of the soul upon God by an unceasing return of love, prayer, and praise.

From this, we may infer the absolute necessity of this continual reaction of the soul upon God in order to the continuance of the divine life in the soul. It plainly appears that God does not continue to act upon the soul unless the soul continues to react upon God.

Praise Brings Provision
ANDREW MURRAY

Receiving from God in faith the answer with perfect assurance that it has been given, is not necessarily the possession of the gift we have asked for. At times there may be a long interval before we have it physically. In other cases we may enjoy at once what we have received. When the interval is long we have need of faith and patience. We need faith to rejoice in the assurance of the answer bestowed and to begin to act upon that answer though for the present there is no visible proof of its presence.

We can apply this principle to our prayer for the power to be faithful intercessors. Hold fast to the divine assurance that as surely as we believe, we receive. Rejoice in the certainty of an answered prayer. The more we praise God for it, the sooner will the experience come. We may begin at once to pray for others in the confidence that grace will be given us to pray with more perseverance and more faith than we have done before.

If we do not find an immediate increase in our desire to pray, this must not discourage us. We have accepted a spiritual gift by faith; in that faith we are to pray, doubting nothing. We may count upon the Holy Spirit to pray in us, even though it is with groanings which cannot find expression. In due time we shall become conscious of His presence and power.

Sacrifice of Praise
John Wesley

God goes before us with the blessings of His goodness. He first loves us and manifests Himself unto us. While we are yet afar off, He calls us to Himself and shines upon our hearts. But if we do not then love Him who first loved us nor hearken to His voice, turn our eye away from Him and not attend to the light which He pours in upon us, His Spirit will not always strive

(Genesis 6:3). He will gradually withdraw and leave us to the darkness of our hearts. He will not continue to breathe into our soul, unless our soul breathes toward Him again, unless we unceasingly return to Him our love, praise, and prayer, the thoughts of our hearts, our words, and works: body, soul, and spirit in a holy, acceptable sacrifice (Romans 12:1).

Songs of Praise
John Wesley

To obey is better than sacrifice.
1 Samuel 15:22

Another passage in which the expression "Stand still" occurs reads thus:

Then some came and told Jehoshaphat, saying, "A great multitude is coming against you from beyond the sea." . . . And Jehoshaphat feared, and set himself to seek the Lord, and proclaimed a fast throughout all Judah. So Judah gathered together to ask help from the Lord; and from all the cities of Judah they came to seek the Lord. Then Jehoshaphat stood in the assembly. . .in the house of the Lord. . . . Then the Spirit of the Lord came upon Jahaziel. . .and he said, "Listen. . .Thus says the Lord to you: Be not afraid nor dismayed by reason of this great multitude. . . . To morrow go ye down against them. . . . Ye shall not need to fight in this battle: set yourselves, stand ye still, and see the salvation of the Lord with you . . . . And they rose early in the morning, and went forth . . . . And when they began to sing and to praise, the Lord set ambushments against the children of Ammon, Moab, and mount Seir. . . .[And] every one helped to destroy another. (2 Chronicles 20:2–5, 14–17, 20, 22–23)

Such was the salvation that the children of Judah saw. They obeyed. *They sang and praised the Lord.*

Worship Impregnated with Prayer
E. M. BOUNDS

God's marvelous, miracle-working times have been times of marvelous, miracle-working praying. The greatest thing in God's worship by His own estimate is praying. Worship's chief service and its distinguishing feature is prayer:

Even them will I bring to my holy mountain, and make them joyful in my house of prayer: their burnt offerings and their sacrifices shall be accepted upon mine altar; for mine house shall be called a house of prayer for all people. (Isaiah 56:7)

This was true under all the gorgeous rites and parade of ceremonies under the Jewish worship. Sacrifice, offering, and the atoning blood were all to be impregnated with prayer. The smoke of burnt offering and perfumed incense which filled God's house was to be but the flame of prayer, and all of God's people were to be anointed priests to minister at His altar of prayer. So all things were to be done with mighty prayer, because mighty prayer was the fruitage and inspiration of mighty faith. But much more is it now true every way under the more simple service of the gospel.

Unceasing Praise
JOHN WESLEY

Rejoice evermore. Pray without ceasing. . . . Give thanks.
1 THESSALONIANS 5:16–18

"*Rejoice evermore*" in uninterrupted happiness in God. "*Pray without ceasing*," which is the fruit of "*always rejoicing*" in the Lord. "*In every thing give thanks,*" which is the fruit of both the former. *This* is Christian perfection. Further than this we cannot go, and we need not stop short of it.

Our Lord has purchased joy, as well as righteousness, for us. It is the very design of the gospel that, being saved from guilt, we should be happy in the love of Christ.

Prayer may be said to be the breath of our spiritual life. One who lives cannot possibly cease breathing. So much as we really enjoy of God's presence, so much prayer and praise do we offer up "*without ceasing*"; else our rejoicing is but delusion.

Thanksgiving is inseparable from true prayer; it is almost essentially connected with it. One who always prays is ever giving praise, whether in ease or pain, both for prosperity and for the greatest adversity. He blesses God for all things, looks on them as coming from Him, and receives them only for His sake—not choosing nor refusing, liking nor disliking, anything, but only as it is agreeable or disagreeable to His perfect will.

"*For this,*" that you should thus rejoice, pray, give thanks, "*is the will of God,*" always good, always pointing at our salvation [1 Thessalonians 5:18]!

Entering In
ANDREW MURRAY

What things soever ye desire, when ye pray, believe that ye receive them, and ye shall have them.
MARK 11:24

The desire of the heart must become the expression of the lips. The Lord Jesus more than once asked those who cried out to Him what they wanted. He wanted them to say what they desired. To declare it brought them into contact with Him and wakened their expectation. To pray is to enter into God's presence, to have distinct dealing with Him, to commit our need to Him and to leave it there. In so doing we become fully conscious of what we are seeking.

There are some who often carry strong desires in their heart but don't bring them to God in a clear expression of repeated prayer. There are others who go to the Word and its promises to strengthen their faith but do not pointedly ask God to fulfill them. Therefore their heart does not gain the assurance that the matter has been put into God's hands. Still others come in prayer with so many requests and desires that it is difficult for them to say what they really expect God to do.

If you want God to give you this gift of faithfulness in prayer and power to pray as you should, begin to pray about it. Declare to yourself and to God.

All That Christ's Presence Implies

ANDREW MURRAY

"I will be with thee."
EXODUS 3:12

When Christ said to His disciples, "All power is given unto me in heaven and in earth," the promise immediately followed, "I am with you always" (Matthew 28:18, 20). The Omnipotent One is truly the Omnipresent One. The writer of Psalm 139 speaks of God's omnipresence as something beyond his comprehension: "Such knowledge is too wonderful for me; it is high, I cannot attain unto it" (verse 6).

The revelation of God's omnipresence in the man Christ Jesus makes the mystery still deeper. The fact that we can experience this presence every moment is inexpressibly wonderful. And yet many of us find it difficult to understand all that Christ's presence implies and how, through prayer, it can become the practical experience of our daily life.

When Christ says "always," He means to give us the assurance that there should never be a moment in which that presence cannot be our experience. Yet, it does not depend upon what we can effect, but upon what He undertakes to do.

The omnipotent Christ is indeed the omnipresent Christ. His promise to us is: "I am with you always." Let your faith in Christ, the Omnipresent One, be in the quiet confidence that He will be with you every day and every moment. Meet Him in prayer, and let His presence be your strength for service.

Prayers as Incense
Andrew Murray

And another angel came and stood at the altar, having a golden censer; and there was given unto him much incense, that he should offer it with the prayers of all saints upon the golden altar which was before the throne. And the smoke of the incense, which came with the prayers of the saints, ascended up before God out of the angel's hand. And the angel took the censer, and filled it with fire of the altar, and cast it into the earth: and there were voices, and thunderings, and lightnings, and an earthquake.
Revelation 8:3–5

The same censer brings the prayer of the saints before God and casts fire upon the earth. The prayers that go up to heaven have their share in the history of this earth. Be sure that thy prayers enter God's presence.

The Chief Thing
Andrew Murray

Worship God.
Revelation 22:9

Why is it that prayer and intercession with God are not a greater joy and delight? One answer to this question undoubtedly is: We know God too little. In our prayer, His presence is not the chief thing our heart is seeking. And yet it should be. Often when we pray, we think mostly of ourselves, our needs, our desires. But we forget that in every prayer, God must be first, must be all.

So how is one to attain this nearness to God and fellowship with Him? The answer is simple: We must give God time to make Himself known to us. Believe with your whole heart, that just as you present yourself to God as a supplicant, so God presents Himself to you as the hearer of prayer. But you cannot realize this unless you give Him time and quiet.

It is not in the multitude or the earnestness of your words in which prayer has its power. Your prayer has its power in the living faith that God Himself is taking you and your prayer into His loving heart. He Himself will give the assurance that in His time your prayer will be heard.

Begin your day with these words: "Unto thee, O LORD, do I lift up my soul" (Psalm 25:1). "My soul thirsteth for God, for the living God" (Psalm 42:2).

Yield to God's Spirit
ANDREW MURRAY

We may think we know what sin is keeping us from prayer, but only God can truly reveal it. For example, after the defeat at Ai, He spoke to Joshua. "Israel hath sinned, and they have also transgressed my covenant" [Joshua 7:11]. Israel had sinned. God himself revealed it.

God must reveal to us that the lack of prayer is a greater sin than we have thought. It means we have little taste for fellowship with God. Our faith rests more on our own work than on the power of God. We are not ready to sacrifice ease for time with God.

When the pressure of work becomes the excuse for not finding time in His presence, there is no sense of absolute dependence upon God. There is no full surrender to Christ.

If we would yield to God's Spirit, all our excuses

would fall away and we would admit that we had sinned. Samuel once said, "As for me, God forbid that I should sin against the LORD in ceasing to pray for you: but I will teach you the good and the right way" (1 Samuel 12:23). Ceasing from prayer is sin against God.

When God discloses sin it must be confessed and cast out. If we have reason to think prayerlessness is the sin that is in "our camp," let us begin with personal and united confession. With God's help let us put away and destroy the sin. Then we can know His presence and power.

Waiting for Jesus
ANDREW MURRAY

Jesus saith unto her, Mary. She turned herself, and saith unto him, Rabboni.
JOHN 20:16

Here we have the first manifestation of the risen Savior—to Mary Magdalene, the woman who loved Jesus so much.

Think of what the morning watch meant to Mary. Is it not a proof of the intense longing of a love that would not rest until it had found the Lord? It meant a separation from all else in her longing to find Christ. It meant the struggle of fear against a faith that refused to let go its hold of Christ's wonderful promise: "He that hath my commandments, and keepeth them, he it is that loveth me: and he that loveth me shall be loved of my Father, and I will love him, and will manifest myself to him" (John 14:21).

That first morning watch, waiting in prayer for the risen Lord to reveal Himself, has been a joy to thousands of souls! With a burning love and strong hope, they wait for Jesus to manifest Himself as the Lord of Glory. There they learn to dwell in the keeping of His abiding presence.

Intense Devotion

ANDREW MURRAY

As he sat at meat with them. . . . their eyes were opened, and they knew him.
LUKE 24:30–31

Mary [Magdalene; see John 20:16] teaches us what the morning watch can mean for the revelation of Jesus to the soul. Emmaus reminds us of the place that the evening prayer has in preparing for the full manifestation of Christ in the soul.

When Jesus Himself approached the two disciples as they traveled, they did not recognize Him. But as the Lord spoke with them, their hearts began to burn within them. Yet they never thought that it might be Christ Himself. How often does Jesus come near with the purpose of manifesting Himself to us, and yet we don't see Him?

When Jesus told the two disciples He must continue on His journey, their plea to spend the night caused Him to stay. We, too, should reserve time toward the end of the day when our whole heart prays with the urgency that constrains Him.

So what was it that led our Lord to reveal Himself to these two men? Nothing less than this: their intense devotion to their Lord. There may be much ignorance and unbelief, but if there is a burning desire that longs for Christ, He will make Himself known to us. In such intense devotion and constraining prayer, the Lord will open our eyes and we will know Him and enjoy the secret of His abiding presence.

The Spirit in Your Own Work

ANDREW MURRAY

I also labour, striving according to his working, which worketh in me mightily.
COLOSSIANS 1:29

You have your own special work; make it a work of intercession. Paul worked hard, depending on God's power working in him. Remember, God not only created us but works in us. You can do your work only in His strength—by Him working in you through the Spirit.

Intercede often for those you work with and for other believers, too. Pray in God's very presence. "Draw nigh to God, and he will draw nigh to you" (James 4:8).

The nearness of God gives rest and power in prayer. The nearness of God is given to those who make it their first aim to "draw nigh to God." Seek His nearness, and He will give it. "He will draw nigh to you." Then it becomes easy to pray in faith.

Remember that when first God takes you into the school of intercession, it is almost more for your own sake than that of others. You have to be trained to love and wait and pray and believe. Only persevere. Learn to place yourself in His presence, to wait quietly for the assurance that He draws near. Enter His holy presence, wait there, and bring your concerns before Him.

The Fulfillment of God's Desires

Andrew Murray

For the LORD hath chosen Zion; he hath desired it for his habitation.

PSALM 132:13

The one great desire of God that moved Him in the work of redemption was that His heart longed for us to dwell with Him and in Him. He said to Moses: "Let them make me a sanctuary; that I may dwell among them" (Exodus 25:8). As His children we are called to yield ourselves to God to dwell in us and to bring others to become His habitation.

What an honor to find our lives and our joy in bringing others to Christ in whom God may find His heart's delight: "Here will I dwell; for I have desired it" [Psalm 132:14].

This is what we can do. We can ask God to give those around us His Holy Spirit. It is God's great plan that we will build Him a habitation. God will give His power and blessing in answer to the unceasing intercession of His children. As this desire of God fills us, we will give ourselves totally to work for its fulfillment.

Let us begin, as never before, to pray for our children, for those around us, and for all the world. Pray not only because we love them but also because God longs for them. He gives us the honor of being the channels through whom His blessing is brought down.

Purpose

God's Purpose, Our Prayers
S. D. GORDON

Prayer does not influence God. Prayer surely does influence God. It does not influence His purpose. It does influence His action. Every right thing that has ever been prayed for God has already purposed to do. But He does nothing without our consent. He has been hindered in His purposes by our lack of willingness. When we learn His purposes and make them our prayers, we are giving Him the opportunity to act. It is a double opportunity: manward and Satanward. We are willing. Our willingness checkmates Satan's opposition. It opens the path to God and rids it of the obstacles, and so the road is cleared for the free action already planned. . . .

The fact that prayer does not make any change in God's thought or purpose reveals His marvelous love in a very tender way.

Suppose I want and *need* something very much, and I go to God and ask for it. And suppose He is reluctant about giving it. But I am insistent, and plead and persist, and by and by God is impressed with my earnestness and sees that I really need the thing, answers my prayer, and gives me what I ask. Is not that a loving God to listen and yield to my plea? Surely.

But suppose God is thinking about me all the time and lovingly planning for me and longing to give me much that He has. Yet in His wisdom He does not give because I do not know my own need and have not opened my hand to receive, and, further, not knowing my need, I might abuse, misuse, or fail to use something given before I felt the need of it. And now I see and feel that need and come and ask and He, delighted with the change in me, eagerly gives. Tell me, is not that a very much more loving God than the other conception suggests? The truth is, *that* is God. Jesus says, "Your Father knoweth what things ye have need of, *before ye ask him*" (Matthew 6:8, emphasis added). And He is a Father. And with God the word *father* means mother, too. Then what He *knows* we need He has *already planned* to give. The great question for me then in praying for some personal thing is this: Do *I* know what *He* knows I need? Am I thinking about what He is thinking about for me? . . .

Prayer does not and cannot change the purpose of such a God. For every right and good thing we might ask for He has already planned to give us. But prayer does change the action of God because He cannot give against our wills, and our willingness as expressed by our asking gives Him the opportunity to do as He has already planned.

No Commonplace Tameness
E. M. Bounds

"He that spared not his own Son, but delivered him up for us all, how shall he not with him also freely give us all things?"

What a basis have we here in Romans 8:32, for prayer and faith, illimitable, measureless in breadth, in depth, and in height! . . . .

No commonplace tameness should restrain our largest asking. Large, larger, and largest asking magnifies grace and adds to God's glory. Feeble asking impoverishes the asker and restrains God's purposes for the greatest good and obscures His glory.

Prayer as Partnership with God
S. D. GORDON

Answers to prayer are delayed or denied out of kindness, *or* that more may be given, *or* that a far larger purpose may be served. But deeper down by far than that is this: *God's purposes are being delayed* because of our unwillingness to learn how to pray, *or* our slowness in learning. It is a small matter that my prayer is answered or unanswered; not small to me, perhaps, but small in proportion. It is a tremendous thing that *God's purpose* for a world is being held back through my lack. The thought that prayer is *getting things* from God is pitiably small and yet so common. The true conception understands that prayer is partnership with God in His planet-sized purposes.

The real reason for the delay or failure lies simply in the difference between God's viewpoint and ours. In our asking we have either not reached the *wisdom* that asks best *or* we have not reached the *unselfishness* that is willing to sacrifice a good thing for a better, or the best, the unselfishness that is willing to sacrifice the smaller personal desire for the larger thing that affects the lives of many.

One Great Purpose
JOHN WESLEY

Your Father knoweth what things ye have need of, before ye ask him.
MATTHEW 6:8

In His words just before those above cited, our Lord had been advising against *vain repetition*. Repeating any words without meaning them is certainly vain repetition. Therefore, we should be extremely careful in all our prayers to mean what we say and to say only what we mean from the bottom of our hearts. The vain and heathenish repetitions which we are here warned against are most dangerous, yet very common. This is a principal cause why so many who still profess religion are a disgrace to it. Indeed, all the words in the world are not equivalent to one holy desire. And the very best prayers are but vain repetitions if they are not the language of the heart.

"And your Father knows what things you have need of." We do not pray to inform God of our wants. Omniscient as He is, He cannot be informed of anything which He did not know before. And He is always willing to relieve our needs. The chief thing lacking is a suitable disposition on our part to receive His grace and blessing. Consequently, one great purpose of prayer is to produce such a disposition in us, to exercise our dependence on God, to increase our desire of the things we ask for, and to make us so sensible of our needs that we never cease wrestling till we have prevailed for the blessing (see Genesis 32:24–30).

Petitions

For Temporal Matters
E. M. BOUNDS

Our temporal matters have much to do with our health

and happiness. They form our relations. They are tests of honesty and belong to the sphere of justice and righteousness. Not to pray about temporal matters is to leave God out of the largest sphere of our being. He who cannot pray in everything, as we are charged to do by Paul in Philippians 4:6, has never learned in any true sense the nature and worth of prayer. To leave business and time out of prayer is to leave religion and eternity out of it. He who does not pray about temporal matters cannot pray with confidence about spiritual matters. He who does not put God by prayer in his struggling toil for daily bread will never put Him in his struggle for heaven.

Nothing Too Great or Small
E. M. BOUNDS

"In every thing. . .let your requests be made known unto God" [Philippians 4:6], says Paul. Nothing is too great to be handled in prayer, or to be sought in prayer. Nothing is too small to be weighed in the secret councils of the closet, and nothing is too little for its final arbitrament. As care comes from every source, so prayer goes to every source. As there are no small things in prayer, so there are no small things with God. He who counts the hairs of our head, and who is not too lofty and high to notice the little sparrow which falls to the ground, is not too great and high to note everything which concerns the happiness, the needs, and the safety of His children. Prayer brings God into what men are pleased to term the little affairs of life. The lives of people are made up of these small matters, and yet how often do great consequences come from small beginnings?

Requests Brought, Peace Given
E. M. BOUNDS

"Let your requests be made known unto God" [Philippians 4:6]. The "requests" must be made known unto God. Silence is not prayer. Prayer is asking God for something which we have not, which we desire, and which He has promised to give in answer to prayer. Prayer is really verbal asking. Words are in prayer. Strong words and true words are found in prayer. Desires in prayer are put into words. The praying one is a pleader. He urges his prayer by arguments, promises, and needs. . . .

"Requests" mean to ask for one's self. The man is in a strait. He needs something, and he needs it badly. Other help has failed. It means a plea for something to be given which has not been done. The request is for the Giver—not alone His gifts but Himself. The requests of the praying one are to be made known unto God. The requests are to be brought to the knowledge of God. It is then that cares fly away, anxieties disappear, worries depart, and the soul gets at ease. Then there steals into the heart "the peace of God, which passeth all understanding" [Philippians 4:7].

Pray with Confidence
ANDREW MURRAY

Holy Father, keep through thine own name those whom thou hast given me. . . . I pray not that thou shouldest take them out of the world, but that thou shouldest keep them from the evil.
JOHN 17:11, 15

Pray that God's people may be kept from the world.

The night before He was crucified, Christ asked three things for His disciples: 1) that they might be kept and cared for as those who are not of the world; 2) that they might be purified; 3) that they might be one in love. You cannot do better than to pray just as Jesus prayed. Ask that God's people may be kept separate from the world and the evil one. Pray that they, by the Holy Spirit, may live as those who are not of the world.

Pray with confidence before God. "Beloved, if our heart condemn us not, then have we confidence toward God. And whatsoever we ask, we receive of him, because we keep his commandments, and do those things that are pleasing in his sight" (1 John 3:21–22).

Memorize that verse. Get the words into your heart. Join the ranks of those who, like John, draw near to God with an assured heart that does not condemn them. Learn to have confidence toward God. In the quiet confidence of an obedient child, pray for those believers who sin (1 John 5:16). Pray for all to be kept from the evil one. And say often, "What we ask, we receive, because we keep and do."

Be Very Definite
ANDREW MURRAY

What wilt thou that I shall do unto thee?
LUKE 18:41

The Lord knew what the man wanted, and yet He asked him. The utterance of our wish gives point to the transaction in which we are engaged with God, and so awakens faith and expectation. Be very definite in your petitions, so as to know what answer you may look for. Just think of the great host of workers, and ask and expect God definitely to bless them in answer to the prayers of His people. Then ask still more definitely for workers around you. Intercession is not the breathing out of pious wishes; its aim is, in believing, persevering prayer, to receive and bring down blessing.

Leave Your Petitions
ANDREW MURRAY

The things that are impossible with men are possible with God. When we think of the great things we ask for, of how little likelihood there is of their coming, of our own insignificance—prayer is not only wishing or asking, but believing and accepting. Be still before God and ask Him to give you to know Him as the almighty One, and leave your petitions with Him who doeth wonders.

Expectations

The Word of God
ANDREW MURRAY

For the word of God is quick, and powerful.
HEBREWS 4:12

When communing with God, His Word and prayer are both indispensable and should not be separated. In His Word, God speaks to me; in prayer, I speak to God.

The Word teaches me to know the God to whom I pray; it teaches me how He would have me pray. It gives me precious promises to encourage me in prayer.

It often gives me wonderful answers to prayer.

The more I pray, the more I feel my need of the Word and rejoice in it. The more I read God's Word, the more I have to pray about and the more power I have in prayer. One great cause of prayerlessness is that we read God's Word too little or only superficially or in the light of human wisdom.

It is the Holy Spirit through whom the Word has been spoken, who is also the Spirit of prayer. He will teach me how to receive the Word and how to approach God.

What power and inspiration would be ours if we only took God's Word as from Himself, turning it into prayer and definitely expecting an answer. It is in the intimacy of God's presence and by the Holy Spirit that God's Word will become our delight and our strength.

Time to Know His Presence
ANDREW MURRAY

Take time when you pray. The psalmist said, "I give myself unto prayer" (Psalm 109:4). The early church leaders agreed. "We will give ourselves continually to prayer" (Acts 6:4). Solomon in his God-given wisdom said, "Be not rash with thy mouth. . . . Let thy words be few" (Ecclesiastes 5:2).

Time is one of the main standards to measure value. The time we give is proof of the interest we feel. We need time with God—to know His presence and to wait for Him to make Himself known. We need time to consider and feel the needs we pray for. We need time to pray until we can believe that we have received.

Encouraged Expectations
E. M. BOUNDS

Mighty is the power of prayer. Wonderful are its fruits. Remarkable things are brought to pass by men of prayer. Many are the wonders of prayer wrought by an Almighty hand. The evidences of prayer's accomplishments almost stagger us. They challenge our faith. They encourage our expectations when we pray.

Expect the Unexpected
ANDREW MURRAY

Ah Lord GOD! behold, thou hast made the heaven and the earth by thy great power. . .there is nothing too hard for thee. . . . Behold, I am the LORD. . .is there any thing too hard for me?
JEREMIAH 32:17, 27

Beware, in your prayer, above everything, of limiting God, not only by unbelief, but by fancying that you know what He can do. Expect unexpected things above all that we ask or think. Each time you intercede, be quiet first and worship God in His glory. Think of what He can do, of how He delights to hear Christ, of your place in Christ; and expect great things.

The Real Victory
S. D. GORDON

The whole circle of endeavor in winning people includes an infinite variety. There is speaking the truth to a number of persons, as well as to one at a time; the doing of kindly acts of helpfulness; teaching; the almost omnipotent ministry of money; letter writing; printer's ink in endless variety. All these are in God's plan for winning men. But the intensely fascinating fact to mark is this: the real victory in all of this service is won in secret, beforehand, by prayer, and these other indispensable things are the moving on the works of the enemy and claiming the victory already won. Then we go into service with a spirit of expectancy that sweeps the field at the start and steadily persists on the stubbornly contested spots until the whipped foe turns tail and runs. Prayer is striking the winning blow at the concealed enemy. Service is gathering up the results of that blow among the people we see and touch. Great patience and tact and persistence are needed in service because each person must be influenced in his own will. But the shrewd strategy that wins puts the secret fighting first.

Confident Expectation
ANDREW MURRAY

Call unto me, and I will answer thee, and shew thee great and mighty things, which thou knowest not.
JEREMIAH 33:3

Thus saith the Lord GOD; I will yet for this be enquired of. . .to do it.
EZEKIEL 36:37

Both texts refer to promises definitely made, but their fulfillment would depend upon prayer: God would be inquired of to do it.

Pray for God's fulfillment of His promises to His Son and His church, and expect the answer.

Expect Great Things
ANDREW MURRAY

Do not limit God in your prayers. It is a fearful thing to do so. "They turned back and tempted God, and limited the Holy One of Israel" (Psalm 78:41). Jesus "did not many mighty works there because of their unbelief" (Matthew 13:58). However, apart from such unbelief, God is not limited. "Is any thing too hard for the LORD?" (Genesis 18:14). "Ah Lord GOD! behold, thou hast made the heaven and the earth by thy great power and stretched out arm, and there is nothing too hard for thee. . . . I am the LORD. . . . Is there anything too hard for me?" (Jeremiah 32:17, 27).

A Wonderful Certainty
ANDREW MURRAY

I will look unto the LORD; I will wait for the God of my salvation: my God will hear me.
MICAH 7:7

God will hear me. What a wonderful certainty! We have God's Word for it. We have thousands of witnesses that have found it true. We have experienced it ourselves. The Son of God came from heaven with the message that if we ask, the Father will give. Christ prayed on earth; now He is in heaven interceding for us. God hears prayer—God delights in hearing our prayer. He has allowed His people to be tried so that they are compelled to cry to Him and learn to know Him as the Hearer of prayer.

We should confess with shame how little we have believed this truth. We have failed to receive it into our hearts. Accepting a truth is not enough; the living God must be revealed by it so that our whole life is spent in His presence. We must live with an awareness as clear as in a little child toward its earthly parent—I know for certain my Father hears me.

By experience you know how little an intellectual understanding of truth has profited you. Ask God to reveal Himself to you. If you want to live a different prayer life, bow to worship God in silence each time before you pray. Wait there until you have a deep consciousness of His nearness and His readiness to answer. After that you can begin to pray with the words, "God will hear me!"

Hindrances

Three Hindrances to Prayer
S. D. GORDON

There are three things directly spoken of in the Bible that hinder prayer. The first one is sin.

. . . There is no trouble on the *up* side. God is all right. "But your *iniquities*. . .your *sins*. . . your *hands*. . . your *fingers*. . .your *lips*. . .your *tongue*. . ." (Isaiah 59:2–3, emphasis added). The slime of sin is oozing over everything! Look at the sixty-sixth Psalm: "If I regard iniquity in my heart, the Lord will not hear" (66:18). How much more if the sin of the heart gets into the hands or the life! *Sin hinders prayer*. There is nothing surprising about this. That we can think the reverse is the surprising thing. Prayer is transacting business with

God. Sin is *breaking with God*. . . .

There is a second thing that hinders prayer. James speaks of it in his letter. "Ye have not, because ye *ask* not" (James 4:2, emphasis added). That explains many parched lives and churches and unsolved problems: no pipelines run up to tap the reservoir and give God an opening into the troubled territory. Then he pushes on to say, "Ye ask *and receive not*" (4:3, emphasis added). Ah! there's the rub; it is evidently an old story, this thing of not receiving. Why? "Because ye ask amiss, that you may consume it *upon your lusts*" (James 4:3, emphasis added). It is selfish praying, asking for something just because I want it for myself. . . .

A third thing spoken of as hindering prayer is an unforgiving spirit. . . . "Well," someone says, "you do not know how hard it is to forgive." You think not? I know this much: some people and some things you *cannot* forgive by yourself. But I also know that if one allows the Spirit of Jesus to sway the heart He will make you love persons you *cannot* like. Jesus' love, when allowed to come in as freely as He means, fills your heart with pity for the person who has wounded you.

But we must forgive freely, frankly, generously if we are to be in prayer touch with God. . . .

Sin, selfishness, an *unforgiving spirit*—what searchlights these words are! God's great love-plan for His prodigal world is being held back and lives being lost because of the lack of human prayer partners.

May we not well pray, "Search me, O God, and know my heart and help me know it. Try me and know my innermost thoughts and purposes and ambitions, and help me know them; and see what way there be in me that is a grief to You. Then lead me out of that way into *Your* way. For Jesus' sake, indeed for men's sake, too" [see Psalm 139:23–24].

Four Striking Instances of Delayed Answers to Prayer
S. D. GORDON

In the Bible there are four striking instances of delayed answers to prayer. There are others, but these stand out sharply and perhaps include the main teachings of all. These four are Moses' request to enter Canaan; Hannah's prayer for a son; Paul's thorn; and Jesus' prayer in Gethsemane. . . .

Many a Hebrew mother told her child of Moses their great leader; his appearance, his majestic mien, yet infinite tenderness and gentleness, his presence with God on the mount, the shining face. And the child would listen quietly, and then the eyes would grow big as the mother would repeat softly, "But he could not come over into the land of promise because *he did not obey God.*" And strong fathers reminded their growing sons. And so *reverent obedience to God* was woven into the warp and woof of the nation. One can well understand Moses looking down from above with grateful heart that he had been denied for *their* sakes. The unselfishness and wisdom of later years would not have made the prayer. *The prayer of a man was denied that a nation might be taught obedience.* . . .

Now let us look at the portrait of Hannah the Hebrew woman. . . .

[God] wanted: *a leader*! But there were no leaders, and there were no men out of whom leaders might be made. And worse yet, *there were no women* of the sort to train and shape a man for leadership. That is the lowest level to which a people can ever get. God had to get a woman before He could get a man. Hannah had in her the making of the woman He needed. God honored her by choosing her, but she had to be changed before she could be used. And so there came those years of pruning and sifting and discipline. And out of those years and experiences there came a new woman, a woman with vision broadened, with spirit mellowed, with strength seasoned, with will so supple as to yield to a higher will, to sacrifice the dearest *personal pleasure* for the worldwide purpose, willing that he who was her dearest treasure should be the nation's *first*.

Then followed months of prayer while the man was coming. Samuel was born, no, farther back yet, was conceived in the atmosphere of prayer and devotion to God. The prenatal influences for those months gave the sort of man God wanted. And a nation, *the* nation, the *world-plan*, was saved! This man became a living answer to prayer. The romantic story of the little boy up in the Shiloh tabernacle quickly spread over the nation. His very name—Samuel, "God hears"—sifted into people's ears the facts of a God and the power of prayer. The very sight of the boy and of the man clear to the end kept deepening the brain impression that God answers prayer. And the seeds of that re-belief in God that Samuel's leadership brought about were sown by the unusual story of his birth.

The answer was delayed that more might be given and gotten.

The third great picture in this group is that of Paul and his needle-pointed thorn. . . .

God had a hard time holding Paul to His plans.

Paul had some of his own. . . .

That is the man. Now for the thorn. Something came into Paul's life that was a constant irritation. He calls it a thorn. . . . He went to God and said, "*Please* take this away." But it stayed. A second time the prayer; a bit more urgent; the thing sticks. The time test is the hardest test of all. Still no change. Then praying the third time with what earnestness one can well imagine.

Now note three things: First, *there was an answer.* God answered the man. Though He did not grant the petition, He answered the man. . . . It was in the lonely vigil of a sleepless night, likely as not, that the wondrous Jesus-Spirit drew near to Paul. "Paul," the voice said, "I know about that thorn—and how it hurts. It hurts Me, too. For *your* sake I would quickly remove it. But Paul, it is a bit better for *others'* sake that it remain; the plan in My heart *through you* for thousands can so best be worked out. I will be so close to your side; you will have such revelations of My glory that the pain will be overlapped; the glory will outstrip the thorn point." . . .

And so out of the experience came a double blessing. There was a much fuller working of God's plan for His poor world. And there was an unspeakable nearness of intimacy with his Lord for Paul. *The man was answered and the petition denied that the larger plan of service might be carried out.*

The last of these pictures is in a room by itself. One enters with a holy hush over his spirit and, with awe, looks at Jesus in Gethsemane. . . .

A bit of that prayer comes to us in tones strangely altered by deepest emotion. "*If it be possible—let this cup pass.*" There is still a clinging to some possibility other than that of this nightmare vision. The strain of spirit almost snaps the life-thread, and a parenthetical prayer for strength goes up. And the angels come with sympathetic strengthening. By and by a calmer mood asserts itself, and out of the darkness a second petition comes. It tells of the tide's turning and the victory full and complete. "*Since this cup may not pass*—since only thus *can* Your great plan for a world be worked out—*Your—will—be—done.*"

The changed prayer was worked out on His knees! There alone with the Father came the clearer understanding of the Father's actual will.

The Great Outside Hindrance: The Traitor Prince
S. D. GORDON

Satan has the power to hold the answer back—for a while. He has not the power to hold it back finally, *if* someone understands and prays with quiet, steady persistence. The real pitch of prayer therefore is toward Satan. . . .

Praying is fighting, spirit-fighting. This old evangelist-missionary-bishop says [in Ephesians 6:11–18] we are in the thick of a fight. There is a war on. How will we best fight? First get into good shape to pray, and then with all your praying strength and skill *pray*. That word *praying* is the climax of this long sentence, and of this whole epistle. This is the sort of action that turns the enemy's flank and reveals his heels. He simply *cannot* stand before persistent knee-work.

Now mark the keenness of Paul's description of the man who does most effective work in praying. There are six qualifications under the figure of the six pieces of armor. A clear understanding of truth, a clean obedient life, earnest service, a simple trust in God, clear assurance of one's own salvation and relation to God, and a good grip of the truth for others—these things prepare a man for the real conflict of prayer. Such a man—praying—drives back these hosts of the traitor prince. Such a man praying is invincible in his Chief, Jesus.

A Double Wrestling Match

Now let us turn to the story of Daniel. In the tenth chapter. . . .

Please notice four things that I think anyone reading this chapter will readily admit. This being talking with Daniel is plainly a spirit being. He is opposed by someone. This opponent plainly must be a spirit being, too, to be resisting a spirit being. Daniel's messenger is from God: that is clear. Then the opponent must be from the opposite camp. And here comes in the strange, unexpected thing: the evil spirit being *has the power to detain God's messenger* for three full weeks by earth's reckoning of time. Then reinforcements come, as we would say. The evil messenger's purpose is defeated, and God's messenger is free to come as originally planned.

There is a double scene being enacted: a scene you can see and a scene you cannot see. An unseen wrestling match in the upper spirit realm, and two embodied spirit beings down on their faces by the river. And both concerned over the same thing.

That is the Daniel story. It is a picture glowing with the action of real life. It is a double picture. Every prayer action is in doubles: a lower human level and an upper spirit level. Many see only the seen and lose heart. While we look at the things that are seen, let us gaze intently at the things unseen; for the seen things are secondary, but the unseen are chief, and the action of life is being decided there.

Prayer Concerns Three

Jesus lets in a flood of light on Satan's relation to prayer in one of His prayer parables. . . "the unjust judge" (see Luke 18:1–8). . . .

Jesus seems so eager that they not miss the meaning here that He departs from His usual habit and says plainly what this parable is meant to teach: "that men ought always to pray, and not to faint." The great essential, He says, is prayer. The great essential in prayer is persistence. The temptation in prayer is that one may lose heart and give up, or give in. . . .

The upshot of the parable is very plain. It contains for us two tremendous truths. First is this: *prayer concerns three*—God to whom we pray, the man on the contested earth who prays, and the evil one against whom we pray. And the purpose of the prayer is not to persuade or influence God but to join forces with Him against the enemy. Not toward God but with God against Satan—that is the main thing to keep in mind in prayer.

The second intense truth is this: the winning quality in prayer is *persistence*. The final test is here. Many who fight well up to this point lose their grip here and lose all. Many who are well equipped for prayer fail here because they have not rightly understood. With clear, ringing tones the Master's voice sounds in our ears again: "men ought always to pray, *and* not to faint."

A Stubborn Foe Routed

. . . Now a look at a word from the Master's lips. It is in the story of the demon-possessed boy, the distressed father, and the defeated disciples [see Matthew 17:14–21; Mark 9:17–29]. . . .

Real, intelligent prayer is what routs Satan's demons, for it routs their chief. David killed the lion and bear in the secret forests before he faced the giant in the open. These disciples were facing the giant in the open without the discipline in secret. "This kind can be compelled to come out by nothing but by prayer" means this: "This kind comes out, and must come out, before the man who prays." This thing that Jesus calls prayer casts out demons. It exerts a positive influence on the hosts of evil spirits. They fear it. They fear the man who becomes skilled in its use.

There are many other passages in the Bible fully as explicit as these. The very language of scripture is full of this truth. But these four great instances are quite sufficient to make the present point clear and plain. This great renegade prince is an actual active factor in the lives of men. He believes in the potency of prayer. He fears it. He can hinder its results for a while. He does his best to hinder it, and to hinder as long as possible.

Prayer Overcomes Him

It defeats his plans and himself. He cannot successfully stand before it. He trembles when some man of simple faith in God prays. Prayer is insistence upon God's will being done. It needs for its practice a man in sympathetic touch with God. Its basis is Jesus' victory. It overcomes the opposing will of the great traitor-leader.

Christ's Commitment
E. M. BOUNDS

Our Lord Jesus Christ is most fully committed to the answer of prayer. "Whatsoever ye shall ask in my name, that will I do, that the Father may be glorified in the Son" (John 14:13). How well assured the answer to prayer is, when that answer is to glorify God the Father! And how eager Jesus Christ is to glorify His Father in heaven! So eager is He to answer prayer which always and everywhere brings glory to the Father, that no prayer offered in His name is denied or overlooked by Him. Says our Lord Jesus Christ again in John 14:14, giving fresh assurance to our faith, "If ye shall ask anything in my name, I will do it." So says He once more, in John 15:7, "Ask what ye will, and it shall be done unto you."

The All-Important Part
E. M. BOUNDS

It is answered prayer which brings praying out of the realm of dry, dead things and makes praying a thing of life and power. It is the answer to prayer which brings things to pass, changes the natural trend of things, and orders all things according to the will of God. It is the answer to prayer which takes praying out of the regions of fanaticism and saves it from being utopian, or from being merely fanciful. It is the answer to prayer which makes praying a power for God and for man and makes praying real and divine. Unanswered prayers are training schools for unbelief, an imposition and a nuisance, an impertinence to God and to man.

Answers to prayer are the only surety that we have prayed aright. . . .

The millions of unanswered prayers are not to be solved by the mystery of God's will. We are not the sport of His sovereign power. He is not playing at "make-believe" in His marvelous promises to answer prayer. The whole explanation is found in our wrong praying. "Ye ask, and receive not, because ye ask amiss" (James 4:3). If all unanswered prayers were dumped into the ocean, they would come very near filling it. Child of God, can you pray? Are your prayers answered? If not, why not? Answered prayer is the proof of your real praying.

The efficacy of prayer from a Bible standpoint lies solely in the answer to prayer. The benefit of prayer has been well and popularly maximized by the saying, "It moves the arm which moves the universe." To get unquestioned answers to prayer is not only important as to the satisfying of our desires, but is the evidence of our abiding in Christ. It becomes more important still. The mere act of praying is no test of our relation to God. The act of praying may be a real dead performance. It may be the routine of habit. But to pray and receive clear answers, not once or twice, but daily, this is the sure test, and is the gracious point of our vital connection with Jesus Christ.

Read our Lord's words from John 15:7 in this connection: "If ye abide in me, and my words abide in you, ye shall ask what ye will, and it shall be done unto you."

To God and to man, the answer to prayer is the all-important part of our praying. The answer to prayer, direct and unmistakable, is the evidence of God's being.

It proves that God lives, that there is a God, an intelligent being, who is interested in His creatures, and who listens to them when they approach Him in prayer. There is no proof so clear and demonstrative that God exists than prayer and its answer. This was Elijah's plea: "Hear me, O Lord, hear me, that this people may know that thou art the Lord God" (1 Kings 18:37).

The answer to prayer is the part of prayer which glorifies God. . . . It is the answer which brings glory to His name.

God Will Not Disappoint
E. M. Bounds

[Jesus] declares in John 16:23–24, as follows:

And in that day ye shall ask me nothing. Verily, verily, I say unto you, Whatsoever ye shall ask the Father in my name, he will give it to you. Hitherto ye have asked nothing in my name. Ask, and ye shall receive, that your joy may be full.

Twice in this passage He declares the answer, pledging His Father, "He will give it to you," and declaring with impressive and most suggestive iteration, "Ask, and ye shall receive." So strong and so often did Jesus declare and repeat the answer as an inducement to pray, and as an inevitable result of prayer, the apostles held it as so fully and invincibly established, that prayer would be answered—and they held it to be their main duty to urge and command men to pray. So firmly were they established as to the truth of the law of prayer as laid down by our Lord, that they were led to affirm that the answer to prayer was involved in and necessarily bound up with all right praying. God the Father and Jesus Christ, His Son, are both strongly committed by all the truth of their word and by the fidelity of their character, to answer prayer.

Not only do these and all the promises pledge Almighty God to answer prayer, but they assure us that the answer will be specific, and that the very thing for which we pray will be given.

Our Lord's invariable teaching was that we receive that for which we ask, obtain that for which we seek, and have that door opened at which we knock. This is according to our heavenly Father's direction to us, and His giving to us for our asking. He will not disappoint us by not answering, neither will He deny us by giving us some other thing for which we have not asked, nor by letting us find some other thing for which we have not sought, nor by opening to us the wrong door, at which we were not knocking. If we ask bread, He will give us bread. If we ask an egg, He will give us an egg. If we ask a fish, He will give us a fish. Not something like bread, but bread itself will be given unto us. Not something like a fish, but a fish will be given. Not evil will be given us in answer to prayer, but good.

Earthly parents, though evil in nature, give for the asking and answer to the crying of their children. The encouragement to prayer is transferred from our earthly father to our heavenly Father, from the evil to the good, to the supremely good; from the weak to the omnipotent, our heavenly Father, centering in Himself all the highest conceptions of fatherhood, abler, readier, and much more than the best, and much more than the ablest earthly father. How much more, who can tell? Much more than our earthly father will He supply all our needs, give us all good things, and enable us to meet every difficult duty and fulfill every law, though hard to flesh and blood, but made easy under the full supply of our Father's beneficent and exhaustless help.

Here we have in symbol and as initial, more than an intimation of the necessity, not only of perseverance in prayer, but of the progressive stages of intentness and effort in the outlay of increasing spiritual force. Asking, seeking, and knocking. Here is an ascending scale from the mere words of asking, to a settled attitude of seeking, resulting in a determined, clamorous and vigorous direct effort of praying.

Just as God has commanded us to pray always, to pray everywhere, and to pray in everything, so He will answer always, everywhere, and in everything.

God has plainly and with directness committed Himself to answer prayer. If we fulfill the conditions of prayer, the answer is bound to come. The laws of nature are not so invariable and so inexorable as the promised answer to pray. The ordinances of nature might fail, but the ordinances of grace can never fail. There are no limitations, no adverse conditions, no weakness, no inability, which can or will hinder the answer to prayer. God's doing for us when we pray has no limitations and is not hedged about by provisos in Himself or in the peculiar circumstances of any particular case. If we really pray, God masters and defies all things and is above all conditions.

Notable Exceptions
E. M. BOUNDS

To give the very thing prayed for and not something

else is fundamental to Christ's law of praying. No prayer for the cure of blind eyes did He ever answer by curing deaf ears. The very thing prayed for is the very thing which He gives. . . .

The illustration and enforcement of the law of prayer are found in the specific answers given to prayer. Gethsemane is the only seeming exception. The prayer of Jesus Christ in that awful hour of darkness and hell was conditioned on these words, "If it be possible, let this cup pass from me." But beyond these utterances of our Lord was the soul and life prayer of the willing, suffering divine victim, "Nevertheless not as I will, but as thou wilt." The prayer was answered, the angel came, strength was imparted, and the meek sufferer in silence drank the bitter cup (Matthew 26:39).

Two cases of unanswered prayer are recorded in the scriptures in addition to the Gethsemane prayer of our Lord. The first was that of David for the life of his baby child, but for good reasons to Almighty God, the request was not granted. The second was that of Paul for the removal of the thorn in the flesh, which was denied. But we are constrained to believe these must have been notable as exceptions to God's rule, as illustrated in the history of prophet, priest, apostle and saint, as recorded in the divine Word. There must have been unrevealed reasons which moved God to veer from His settled and fixed rule to answer prayer by giving the specific thing prayed for.

Waiting May Bring Blessing
ANDREW MURRAY

Pray without ceasing.
1 THESSALONIANS 5:17

One of the greatest drawbacks to the life of prayer is that the answer does not come as quickly as we expect. We are discouraged and think: "Perhaps I do not pray right." So we do not persevere. Jesus often talked about this. There may be a reason for the delay, and the waiting may bring a blessing. Our desire must grow deeper and stronger, and we must ask with our whole heart. God puts us into the practicing school of persevering prayer so that our weak faith may be strengthened.

Above all God wants to draw us into closer fellowship with Him. When our prayers are not answered we learn that the fellowship and love of God are more to us than the answers of our requests, and then we continue in prayer.

Do not be impatient or discouraged if the answer does not come. "Always be prayerful." "Keep on praying." You will find real blessing in doing so. Ask whether your prayer is really in accordance with the will of God and the Word of God. Ask if it is in the right spirit and in the name of Christ. You will learn that the delay in the answer is one of the most precious ways God gives you His grace.

Those who have persevered before God are those who have had the greatest power in prayer.

God Readily Grants Requests
E. M. BOUNDS

We have this case among many in the Old Testament:

Jabez called on the God of Israel, saying, O that thou wouldest bless me indeed, and enlarge my coast, and that thine hand might be with me, and that thou wouldest keep me from evil,

And God readily granted him the things which he had requested.

Hannah, distressed in soul because she was childless and desiring a man child, repaired to the house of prayer and prayed, and this is the record she makes of the direct answer she received: "For this child I prayed; and the LORD hath given me my petition which I asked of him" (1 Samuel 1:27).

Proof

An Illustrious Record
E. M. BOUNDS

And what shall I more say? for the time would fail me to tell of Gedeon, and of Barak, and of Samson, and of Jephthae; of David also, and Samuel, and of the prophets: Who through faith subdued kingdoms, wrought righteousness, obtained promises, stopped the mouths of lions. Quenched the violence of fire, escaped the edge of the sword, out of weakness were made strong, waxed valiant in fight, turned to flight the armies of the aliens. Women received their dead raised to life again: and others were tortured, not accepting deliverance; that they might obtain a better resurrection [Hebrews 11:32–35].

What an illustrious record is this! What marvelous accomplishments, wrought not by armies, or by man's superhuman strength, nor by magic, but all accomplished simply by men and women noted alone for their faith and prayer! Hand in hand with these records of faith's illimitable range are the illustrious records of prayer, for they are all one. Faith has never won a victory nor gained a crown where prayer was not the weapon of the victory, and where prayer did not jewel the crown. If "all things are possible to him that believeth" (Mark 9:23), then all things are possible to him that prayeth.

Proof in Bible Days

Convincing Proof
E. M. BOUNDS

Answer to prayer is the convincing proof of our right relations to God. Jesus said at the grave of Lazarus in John 11:41–42:

Father, I thank thee that thou hast heard me. And I knew that thou hearest me always: but because of the people which stand by I said it, that they may believe that thou hast sent me.

The answer of His prayer was the proof of His mission from God, as the answer to Elijah's prayer was made to the woman whose son he raised to life. She said in 1 Kings 17:24, "Now by this I know that thou art a man of God." He is highest in the favor of God who has the readiest access and the greatest number of answers to prayer from Almighty God.

Instances of Prayer Miracles

E. M. Bounds

If we turn back to Old Testament times, we have no lack of instances of prayer miracles. The saints of those days were well acquainted with the power of prayer to move God to do great things. Natural laws did not stand in the way of Almighty God when He was appealed to by His praying ones. What a marvelous record is that of Moses as those successive plagues were visited upon Egypt in the effort to make Pharaoh let the children of Israel go that they might serve God! As one after another of these plagues came, Pharaoh would beseech Moses, "Intreat the LORD your God, that he may take away from me this death" (Exodus 10:17). And as the plagues themselves were miracles, prayer removed them as quickly as they were sent by Almighty God. The same hand which sent these destructive agencies upon Egypt was moved by the prayers of His servant Moses to remove these same plagues. And the removal of the plagues in answer to prayer was as remarkable a display of divine power as was the sending of the plagues in the first instance. The removal in answer to prayer would do as much to show God's being and His power as would the plagues themselves. They were miracles of prayer.

All down the line in Old Testament days we see these prayer miracles. God's praying servants had not the least doubt that prayer would work marvelous results and bring the supernatural into the affairs of earth. Miracles and prayer went hand in hand. They were companions. The one was the cause, the other was the effect. The one brought the other into existence. The miracle was the proof that God heard and answered prayer. The miracle was the divine demonstration that God, who was in heaven, interfered in earth's affairs, intervened to help men, and worked supernaturally if need be to accomplish His purposes in answer to prayer.

Passing to the days of the early church, we find the same divine record of prayer miracles. The sad news came to Peter that Dorcas was dead and he was wanted at Joppa. Promptly he made his way to that place. Peter put everybody out of the room, and then he kneeled down and prayed, and with faith said, "Tabitha, arise," and she opened her eyes and sat up. Knee work on the part of Peter did the work. Prayer brought things to pass and saved Dorcas for further work on earth (Acts 9:36–43).

In Acts 28, Paul was on that noted journey to Rome under guard and had been shipwrecked on an island. The chief man of the island was Publius, and his old father was critically ill of a bloody flux. Paul laid his hands on the old man and prayed for him, and God came to the rescue and healed the sick man. Prayer brought the thing desired to pass. God interfered with the laws of nature, either suspending or setting them aside for a season, and answered the prayer of this praying servant of His. And the answer to prayer among those heathen people convinced them that a supernatural power was at work among them. In fact, so true was this that they seemed to think a supernatural being had come among them.

In Acts, chapter 12, Peter was put in prison by Herod, after Herod had killed James with the sword. The young church was greatly concerned, but they neither lost heart nor gave themselves over to needless fretting and worrying. They had learned before this from whence their help came. They had been schooled in the lesson of prayer. God had intervened before in the behalf of His servants and interfered when His cause was at stake. "Prayer was made without ceasing of the church unto God for him." An angel on swift wings came to the rescue and, in a marvelous and supernatural way, released Peter and left the prison doors locked. Locks and prison doors and an unfriendly king cannot stand in the way of Almighty God when His people cry in prayer unto Him. Miracles if need be will be wrought in their behalf to fulfill His promises and to carry forward His plans. After this order does the Word of God illustrate and enlarge and confirm the possibilities of prayer. . . .

How quickly to our straits follow our enlargements! God wrought a wonderful work through Samson in Judges 15 in enabling him with a crude instrument, the jawbone of an ass, to slay a thousand men, giving him a great deliverance. Shortly afterward, he was abnormally thirsty, and he was unable to obtain any water. It seemed as if he would perish with thirst. God had saved him from the hands of the Philistines. Could he not as well save him from thirst? So Samson cried unto the Lord, and "God clave an hollow place that was in the jaw, and there came water thereout; and when he had drunk, his spirit came again, and he revived" (Judges 15:19). God could bring water out of the jawbone just as well as He could give victory by it to Samson. God could change that which had been death-dealing to His enemies and make it life-giving to His servant. God can and will work a miracle in answer to prayer in order to deliver His friends, sooner than He will work one to destroy His enemies. He does both, however, in answer to prayer.

Proof in Present Day

Not Without Witness
E. M. BOUNDS

As often as God manifested His power in scriptural times in working wonders through prayer, He has not left Himself without witness in modern times. Prayer brings the Holy Spirit upon men today in answer to importunate, continued prayer just as it did before Pentecost. The wonders of prayer have not ceased.

God Is Still "Mighty to Save"
JOHN WESLEY

When penitent seekers know there is yet forgiveness with God, they will cry aloud that He would blot out their sins also, through faith which is in Jesus. And if they earnestly cry and faint not, if they seek Him in all the means He has appointed, if they refuse to be comforted till He come, He will come, and will not tarry (Hebrews 10:37). And He can do much work in a short time.

The Acts of the Apostles records many examples of God's working this faith in men's and women's hearts, even like lightning falling from heaven. In the same hour that Paul and Silas began to preach, the jailer repented, believed, and was baptized. It was the same with the three thousand on the day of Pentecost who repented and believed at St. Peter's first preaching. And, blessed be God, there are now many living proofs that God is still "mighty to save."

A Matter of Record
E. M. Bounds

The work of George Müller in Bristol, England, was a miracle of the nineteenth century. It will take the opening of the books at the great judgment day to disclose all he wrought through prayer. His orphanage, in which hundreds of fatherless and motherless children were cared for, to sustain which this godly man never asked anyone for money with which to pay its running expenses, is a marvel of modern times. His practice was always to ask God for just what was needed, and the answers which came to him read like a record of apostolic times. He prayed for everything and trusted implicitly to God to supply all his needs. And it is a matter of record that never did he and the orphans ever lack for any good thing.

Some Hidden Secret behind the Power

One of the most remarkable illustrations of the power of prayer may be found in an experience of D. L. Moody. It explains his unparalleled career of worldwide soul winning. One marvels that more has not been said of it. Its stimulus to faith is great. I suppose the man most concerned did not speak of it much because of his humility. The last year of his life he referred to it more frequently as though impelled to.

The last time I heard Mr. Moody was in his own church in Chicago. It was, I think, in the fall of the last year of his life. In a quiet, conversational way he told the story.

Back in the early 1870s he went to London to learn what he could from preachers there, so as to do better work here. He had not been speaking anywhere but listening to others. One Saturday at noon he had gone into a meeting in Exeter Hall on the Strand. He felt compelled to speak a little when the meeting was thrown open, and did so. At the close, a minister asked him to come and preach for him the next day, and he said he would. Mr. Moody said, "I went to the morning service and found a large church full of people. And when the time came I began to speak to them. But it seemed the hardest talking I ever did. There was no response in their faces. They seemed as though carved out of stone or ice. I was having a hard time and wished I wasn't there and wished I hadn't promised to speak again at night. But I had promised, and so I went.

"At night it was the same thing: house full, people outwardly respectful, but no interest, no response. And I was having a hard time again. About halfway through my talk there came a change. It seemed as though the windows of heaven had opened and a bit of breath blew down. The atmosphere of the building seemed to change. The people's faces changed. It impressed me so that when I finished speaking I gave the invitation for those who wanted to be Christians to rise. I thought there might be a few. And to my immense surprise the people got up in groups, pew-fulls. I turned to the minister and said, 'What does this mean?' He said, 'I don't know.'

"Well," Mr. Moody said, "they misunderstood me. I'll explain what I meant." So he announced an after-meeting in the room below, explaining who were invited—only those who wanted to be Christians—and dismissed the service.

They went to the lower room. And the people came crowding in, filling every available space. Mr. Moody talked a few minutes and then asked those who wanted to be Christians to rise. This time he knew he had made his meaning clear. They got up in groups, by fifties! Mr. Moody said, "I turned and said to the minister, 'What *does* this mean?' He said, 'I'm sure I don't know.'" Then the minister said to Mr. Moody, "What'll I do with these people? I don't know what to do with them; this is something new." And he said, "Well, I'd announce a meeting for tomorrow night and Tuesday night, and see what comes of it; I'm going across the channel to Dublin." And he went, but he had barely stepped off the boat when a cablegram was handed him from the minister saying, "Come back at once. Church packed." So he went back and stayed ten days. And the result of that ten days was that four hundred were added to that church, and that every church nearby felt the impulse of those ten days. Then Mr. Moody dropped his head, as though thinking back, and said: "I had no plans beyond this church. I supposed my life work was here. But the result with me was that I was given a roving commission and have been working under it ever since."

Now what was the explanation for that marvelous Sunday and days following? It was not Mr. Moody's doing, though he was a leader whom God could and did mightily use. It was not the minister's doing, for he was as greatly surprised as the leader. There was some secret hidden beneath the surface of those ten days. With his usual keenness Mr. Moody set himself to ferret it out.

By and by this incident came to him. A woman in the church had gotten sick some time before. Gradually she grew worse, until the physician told her that she would not recover. She would not die at once, but she would be a shut-in for years. She lay there trying to think what that meant: to be shut in for years. And she thought of her life and said, "How little I've done for God, practically nothing; and now what can I do shut in here on my back?" And she said, "I can pray. I *will* pray." And she was led to pray for her church. Her sister, also a member of the church, lived with her and was her link with the outer world. Sundays, after church service, the sick woman would ask, "Any special interest in church today?" "No," was the constant reply. Wednesday nights, after prayer meetings, "Any special interest in the service tonight? There must have been." "No; nothing new; same old deacons made the same old prayers."

But one Sunday noon the sister came in from service and asked, "Who do you think preached today?" "I don't know, who?" "Why, a stranger from America, a man called Moody, I think was the name." And the sick woman's face turned a bit whiter and her lip trembled a bit, and she quietly said: "I know what that means. There's something coming to the old church. Don't bring me any dinner. I must spend this afternoon in prayer." And so she did. And that night in the service that startling change came.

Then to Mr. Moody himself, as he sought her out in her sickroom, she told how nearly two years before there came into her hands a copy of a paper published in Chicago called *The Watchman* that contained a talk by Mr. Moody in one of the Chicago meetings. All she knew was that talk made her heart burn, and there was the name Moody. And she was led to pray that God would send that man into their church in London. As simple a prayer as that.

The months went by, and a year, and more; still she prayed. Nobody knew of it but herself and God. No change seemed to come. Still she prayed. And of course her prayer wrought its purpose. Every Spirit-suggested prayer does. The Spirit of God moved that man of God across the water to London and into their church. Then a bit of special siege-prayer, and that night the victory came.

I believe without a doubt that some day when the night is gone and the morning light comes up, we shall find that the largest single factor in that ten days' work and in the changing of tens of thousands of lives under Moody's leadership is that woman in her praying. Not the only factor, mind you. Moody was a man of rare leadership and consecration, and hundreds of faithful ministers and others rallied to his support. But behind and beneath Moody and the others, and to be reckoned with as first, was this woman's praying.

WHEN

When should you pray? Morning, noontime, evening, nighttime? And for how long? These questions seem to plague Christians past and present. As you read, ask God to help you find your way into His secret place, time and time again.

Time to Take Your Place
ANDREW MURRAY

And [He] continued all night in prayer to God.
LUKE 6:12

Time is one of the chief standards of value. The time we give is a proof of the interest we feel.

We need time with God—to realize His presence; to wait for Him to make Himself known; to consider and feel the needs we plead for; to take our place in Christ; to pray 'til we can believe that we have received. Take time in prayer, and pray down blessing.

Time Will Come of Its Own Accord
ANDREW MURRAY

What, could ye not watch with me one hour?
MATTHEW 26:40

Every minute spent in prayer is valuable. If ten minutes is all the time you can give, see what you can do in that time. Most people can spare more time. If you will only persevere from day to day, time will come of its own accord.

Is it possible that Christians can say that they cannot afford to spend a quarter or half an hour alone with God and His Word? When a friend comes to see us or we have to attend an important meeting or there is anything to our advantage or pleasure, we find time easily enough.

But God has a right to us and longs for us to spend time with Him, and we find no time for fellowship with Him. Even God's own servants are so occupied with their own work that they find little time for that which is all-important—waiting on God to receive power from on high.

Dear child of God, let us never say "I have no time for God." Let the Holy Spirit teach us that the most important and profitable time of the whole day is the time we spend alone with God. Communion with God through His Word and prayer is as indispensable to us as the food we eat and the air we breathe. Whatever else is left undone, God has the first and foremost right to our time.

Quiet Time Daily
S. D. Gordon

We need *time* for prayer, unhurried, daily time. I do not mean rising in the morning at the very last moment and dressing hurriedly, and then kneeling a few moments so as to feel easier in mind. I do not mean the last thing at night when you are exhausted and almost between the sheets, and then remember and look up a verse and kneel a few moments. That is good so far as it goes. I am not criticizing that. Better sweeten and sandwich the day with all of that sort you can get in. But right now I mean this: *taking time* to thoughtfully pray when the mind is fresh and alert and the spirit sensitive. We haven't time. Life is so crowded. It must be taken from something else, something important, but still less important than this.

Sacrifice is the continual law of life. The important thing must be sacrificed to the more important. One needs to cultivate a mature judgment or his strength will fizzle out in the less important details and the greater thing go undone, or be done poorly. If we would become skilled intercessors and know how to pray simply enough, we must take quiet time daily to get off alone.

Focus Daily
Andrew Murray

Christ is in me. What a difference it would make if we could take time every morning to focus on the thought: *Christ is in me.*

Christ made it clear to His disciples. The Spirit would teach them: "Yet a little while, and the world seeth me no more; but ye see me: because I live, ye shall live also. At that day ye shall know that I am in my Father, and ye in me, and I in you" (John 14:19–20). Through the power of God we who believe were crucified with Christ and raised again with Him. As a result Christ is in us! Through faith in God's Word, the Christian accepts it.

Paul expresses this thought in the prayer of Ephesians 3:16: "That he would grant you, according to the riches of his glory, to be strengthened with might by his Spirit in the inner man." Notice that it is not the ordinary gift of grace, but a special revelation of the riches of His love that Christ may dwell in your heart by faith. Have you been able to grasp that?

Paul said: "I bow my knees unto the Father" (Ephesians 3:14). That is the only way to obtain the blessing. Take time in prayer in His presence to realize: "Christ dwells in me." Even in the midst of your daily schedule, look upon your heart as the dwelling place of the Son of God. Then Christ's words: "He that abideth in me, and I in him, the same bringeth forth much fruit" (John 15:5) will become your daily experience.

Early Morning Prayer

JOHN WESLEY

Early will I seek thee.
PSALM 63:1

How do you begin your day? Most Christians, if they are not obliged to work for their living, rise at eight or nine in the morning after eight, nine, or more hours of sleep. I do not say (as I was apt to do fifty years ago) all who do this are on the way to hell. But neither can I say they are on the way to heaven, denying themselves and taking up their cross daily. From more than sixty years' observation, I can say that men in health require an average of six to seven hours of sleep and healthy women from seven to eight each twenty-four hours. This quantity of sleep is advantageous to body and soul, preferable to any medicine I have known, both for preventing and removing nervous disorders. In defiance of fashion and custom, it is, therefore, the most excellent way to take just so much sleep as experience proves our nature to require. It is indisputably most conducive both to bodily and spiritual health.

And why should you not? Because it is difficult? True; with men it is impossible. But all things are possible with God; and by His grace, all things will be possible to you. Only be always ready to pray and it will be not only possible, but easy. And, it is far easier to rise early always than only sometimes. Just begin at the right end: To rise early, you must sleep early. Then the difficulty will cease. Its advantage will remain forever.

First Place

ANDREW MURRAY

At a ministerial meeting the superintendent of a large district said: "I rise in the morning and have half an hour with God. I am occupied all day with numerous engagements. Not many minutes elapse without my breathing a prayer for guidance. After work I speak to God of the day's work. But I know little of the intense prayer of which Scripture speaks."

There are earnest Christians who have just enough prayer to maintain their spiritual position but not enough to grow spiritually. Seeking to fight off temptation is a defensive attitude rather than an assertive one which reaches for higher attainment. The scriptural teaching to cry out day and night in prayer must, to some degree, become our experience if we are to be intercessors.

A man said to me, "I see the importance of much prayer, and yet my life hardly allows time for it. Am I to give up? How can I accomplish what I desire?"

I admitted that the difficulty was universal and quoted a Dutch proverb: "What is heaviest must weigh heaviest." The most important must have the first place. The law of God is unchangeable. In our communication with heaven, we only get as we give. Unless we are willing to pay the price—to sacrifice time and attention and seemingly necessary tasks for the sake of the heavenly gifts—we cannot expect much power from heaven in our work.

Morning by Morning
ANDREW MURRAY

My voice shalt thou hear in the morning, O LORD; in the morning will I direct my prayer unto thee, and will look up.
PSALM 5:3

Many Christians observe the morning watch, while others speak of it as the quiet hour, the still hour, or the quiet time. All these, whether they think of a whole hour or half an hour or a quarter of an hour, agree with the psalmist.

In speaking of the extreme importance of this daily time of quiet for prayer and meditation on God's Word, a well-known Christian leader has said: "Next to receiving Christ as Savior and claiming the baptism of the Holy Spirit, we know of no act that brings greater good to ourselves or others than the determination to keep the morning watch and spend the first half hour of the day alone with God."

At first glance this statement appears too strong. The firm determination to keep the morning watch hardly appears sufficiently important to be compared to receiving Christ and the baptism of the Holy Spirit. However, it is true that it is impossible to live our daily Christian life, or maintain a walk in the leading and power of the Holy Spirit, without a daily, close fellowship with God. The morning watch is the key to maintaining a position of total surrender to Christ and the Holy Spirit.

We as believers cannot stand for one moment without Christ. Personal devotion to Him refuses to be content with anything less than to abide always in His love and His will. This is the true scriptural Christian life. The importance, joy, and purpose of the morning watch can only be realized as our personal devotion becomes its chief purpose.

Wholehearted Determination
ANDREW MURRAY

Daniel. . .kneeled upon his knees three times a day, and prayed, and gave thanks before his God, as he did aforetime.
DANIEL 6:10

As we seek to have unbroken fellowship with God in Christ throughout the day, we will realize that only a definite meeting time with Christ will secure His presence for the day. The essential thing to having a daily quiet time is wholehearted determination, whatever effort or self-denial it may cost. In academic study or athletics, every student needs determined purpose to succeed. Christianity requires, and indeed deserves, not less but more intense devotion. If anything, surely the love of Christ needs the whole heart.

When we make this decision to secure Christ's presence, we will overcome every temptation to be superficial in the keeping of our pledges. Our determination will make the morning watch itself a mighty force in strengthening our character and giving us boldness to resist self-indulgence. It will enable us to enter the inner chamber and shut the door for our communion with Christ. From the morning watch on, this firm resolution will become the keynote of our daily life.

Often we hear the statement that great things are possible to those who know what they want and will it with all their heart. If we have made personal devotion to Christ our goal, we will find the morning hour the place where daily insight into our holy calling is renewed. During this quiet time, we are fortified to walk worthy of His calling. Faith is rewarded by the presence of Christ who is waiting to meet us and take charge of us for the day.

We are more than conquerors through Him who loves us. Christ waits to meet us.

Half an Hour of Silence in Heaven
ANDREW MURRAY

There was silence in heaven about the space of half an hour. . . . And there was given unto him much incense, that he should offer it with the prayers of all saints.
REVELATION 8:1, 3

There was silence in heaven for about half an hour— to bring the prayers of the saints before God. Many of God's children have also felt the absolute need of silence and withdrawal from the things of earth for half an hour—to present their prayers before God. In so doing, they have been strengthened for their daily work.

How often the complaint is heard that there is no time for prayer. Yet often the confession is made that, even if time could be found, one feels unable to spend the time in real communion with God. Don't think, "I will not know how to spend the time." Just believe that, if you bow in silence before God, He will reveal Himself to you.

If you need help, read some passages of Scripture and let God's Word speak to you. Then bow in deepest humility before God and wait on Him. He will begin to work within you as you intercede for those whom He has laid on your heart. Keep praying, though the time may seem long. God will surely meet you.

Is it not worth the trouble to take half an hour alone with God? In heaven itself there was need for half an hour's silence to present the prayers of the saints before God. If you persevere, you may find the half-hour that seems the most difficult may become the most blessed in your whole life.

WHERE

Coming into God's presence is an amazingly high privilege. Once the petitioner has entered into that secret place—mentally, physically, spiritually, and emotionally—God wants his or her full attention. Thus, the place of prayer is very important. Read the following carefully and then examine your own place of prayer, making adjustments as God directs.

To the Closet
E. M. BOUNDS

It is to the closet Paul directs us to go. The unfailing remedy for all burdensome, distressing care is prayer. The place where the Lord is at hand is the closet of prayer. There He is always found, and there He is at hand to bless, to deliver, and to help. The one place where the Lord's presence and power will be more fully realized than any other place is the closet of prayer.

Into a Mountain Alone with God
ANDREW MURRAY

He was alone praying...
LUKE 9:18

Jesus...departed again into a mountain himself alone.
JOHN 6:15

Human beings need to be alone with God. Our fall consisted in our being brought, through the lust of the flesh and the world, under the power of things visible and temporal. Our restoration through salvation is meant to bring us back to the Father's love and fellowship.

We need to be alone with God, to yield ourselves to the presence and the power of His holiness. Christ on earth needed it. He could not live the life of a Son here in the flesh without at times separating Himself entirely from His surroundings and being alone with God. How much more must this be indispensable to us!

Alone with God—that is the secret of true power in prayer. There is no true holiness, no clothing with the Holy Spirit and with power, without being alone daily with God.

When our Lord Jesus gave us the command to pray to our Father in secret, He gave us the promise that the Father would hear such prayers and mightily answer them in our life before others. What a privilege it is to begin every morning with intimate prayer. Let it be the one thing our hearts are set on—seeing, finding, and meeting God alone. The time will come when you will be amazed at the thought that one could suggest five minutes was enough.

Through Your Personality
S. D. Gordon

No matter where you are you do more through your praying than through your personality. If you were in India you could *add your personality to your prayer.* That would be a great thing to do. But whether there or here, you must first win the victory, every step, every life, every foot of the way, in secret, in the spirit-realm, and then add the mighty touch of your personality in service. You can do *more* than pray, *after* you have prayed. But you can *not* do more than pray *until* you have prayed. And that is where we have all seemed to make a slip at times. We think we can do more where we are through our service than prayer to give power to service. *No*, we can do nothing of real power until we have done the prayer thing.

Here is a man by my side. I can talk to him. I can bring my personality to bear upon him, that I may win him. But before I can influence his will at all for God, I must first have won the victory in the secret place. Intercession is winning the victory over the chief, and service is taking the field after the chief is driven off. Such service is limited by the limitation of personality to one place.

Court Attendance
E. M. BOUNDS

Sometimes loud words are in prayer. The psalmist said, "Evening, and morning, and at noon, will I pray, and cry aloud" (Psalm 55:17). The praying one wants something which he has not got. He wants something which God has in His possession, and which he can get by praying. He is beggared, bewildered, oppressed, and confused. He is before God in supplication, in prayer, and in thanksgiving. These are the attitudes, the incense, the paraphernalia, and the fashion of this hour, the court attendance of his soul before God.

That Door Is Important
S. D. GORDON

Oh, you can pray anywhere, but you are not likely

to unless you have been off in some quiet place shut in alone with God. The Master said, "Enter into thy closet, and when thou hast shut thy door"—that door is important; it shuts out and it shuts in—"pray to thy Father which is in secret" (Matthew 6:6). God is here in this shut-in spot. One must get alone to find out that he is never alone. The more alone we are as far as people are concerned, the least alone we are so far as God is concerned.

The quiet place and time are needful to train the ears for keen hearing. A quiet place shuts out the outer sounds and gives the inner ear a chance to learn other sounds.

A man was standing in a telephone booth trying to talk but could not make out the message. He kept saying, "I can't hear!" The other man finally said sharply, "If you'll shut that door you can hear." *His* door was shut and he could hear not only the man's voice but the street and store noises, too. Some folks have gotten their hearing badly confused because their doors have not been shut enough. Man's voice and God's voice get mixed in their ears. They cannot distinguish between them. The problem is partly with the door. If you'll shut that door you can hear.

In Secret

Andrew Murray

Have you ever thought what a wonderful privilege it is to have the liberty of asking God to meet with you and to hear what you have to say? We should use such a privilege gladly and faithfully.

"When thou prayest," says Jesus, "enter into thy

closet, and when thou hast shut thy door, pray to thy Father which is in secret" [Matthew 6:6]. This means two things. 1) Shut the world out; withdraw from all the thoughts and concerns of the day. 2) Shut yourself in alone with God to pray in secret. Let this be your chief object in prayer, to realize the presence of your heavenly Father. Let your goal be: "Alone with God."

Being alone in His presence and praying to the Father in secret is only the beginning. Come to Him in the full assurance that He knows how you long for His help and guidance. He will listen to you.

Then follows the great promise of verse 6: "And thy Father which seeth in secret shall reward thee openly." Your Father will see to it that your prayer is not in vain. Prayer in secret will be followed by the secret working of God in my heart.

Go into Your Room

John Wesley

All who desire the grace of God are to wait for it, first, in the way of prayer. This is the express direction of our Lord Himself. In His Sermon on the Mount, after explaining at length of what religion consists and describing the main branches of it, He adds, "Ask, and it shall be given you; seek, and ye shall find; knock, and it shall be opened unto you: for every one that asketh receiveth; and he that seeketh findeth; and to him that knocketh it shall be opened" (Matthew 7:7–8; Luke 11:9–10). In the plainest manner, we are here directed to ask in order to receive, or as a means of receiving; to seek, in order to find the grace of God, the pearl of great price; and to knock, to continue asking and seeking, if we would enter into His kingdom.

That no doubt might remain, our Lord gives a peculiar parable of a father who desires to give good gifts to his children, concluding with these words, "How much more shall your heavenly Father give the Holy Spirit to them that ask him?" (Luke 11:13).

Jesus gives a direction to pray, with a positive promise that by this means we shall obtain our request: "Enter into thy closet, and. . .pray to thy Father which is in secret; and [He]. . .shall reward thee openly" (Matthew 6:6).

Entering the Inner Chamber
ANDREW MURRAY

When he came down from the mount. . .Moses wist not that the skin of his face shone while he talked with him.
EXODUS 34:29

Close and continued prayer fellowship with God will in due time leave its mark and be evident to those around us. Just as Moses did not know that his face shone, we ourselves will be unaware of the light of God shining from us. The sense of God's presence in us may often cause others to feel ill at ease in our company. However, true believers will prove by humility and love that they are indeed persons like those around them. And yet there will be the proof that they are people of God who live in an unseen world.

The blessings of communion with God can easily be lost by entering too deeply into communion with people. The spirit of inner prayer must be carried over into a holy watchfulness throughout the day. We do not know at what hour the enemy will come. This continuance of the morning watch can be maintained by quiet self-restraint, by not giving the reins of our lives over to our natural impulses.

When the abiding sense of God's presence has become the aim of the morning hour, then with deep humility and in loving conversation with those around us, we will pass on into the day's duties with the continuity of unbroken fellowship. It is a great thing to enter the inner chamber, shut the door, and meet the Father in secret. It is a greater thing to open the door again and go out to enjoy God's presence—which nothing can disturb.

Why pray? For all the reasons already covered in the foregoing readings, including, but not limited to, gaining peace beyond understanding; fellowshipping with the great Creator; taking hold of the most amazing, heaven-and-earth-moving privilege and power a believer has been given; and so many others beside. Why pray *and* fast? To get even closer in communion with God. As you read the following, examine your own motivations to pray. Then ask God to help you hone in on even more!

Consolation
JOHN WESLEY

On every occasion of uneasiness, we should retire to prayer, that we may give place to the grace and light of God and then form our resolutions, without being in any pain about what success they may have.

The Divine Injunction
E. M. BOUNDS

We have one of the most important, far-reaching, peace-giving, necessary, and practical prayer possibilities in Paul's words in Philippians 4:6–7, dealing with prayer as a cure for undue care:

Be careful for nothing; but in every thing by prayer and supplication with thanksgiving let your requests be made known unto God. And the peace of God, which passeth all understanding, shall keep your hearts and minds through Christ Jesus.

Ours is an anxious world, and ours is an anxious race. The caution of Paul is well addressed, "In nothing be anxious." This is the divine injunction, and that we might be able to live above anxiety and freed from undue care, "in every thing by prayer and supplication with thanksgiving let your requests be made known unto God." This is the divinely prescribed remedy for all anxious cares, for all worry, for all inward fretting. . . .

Prayer over everything can quiet every distraction, hush every anxiety, and lift every care from care-enslaved lives and from care-bewildered hearts. The prayer specific is the perfect cure for all ills of this character which belong to anxieties, cares, and worries. Only prayer in everything can drive dull care away, relieve unnecessary heart burdens, and save from the besetting sin of worrying over things which we cannot help. Only prayer can bring into the heart and mind the peace "which passeth all understanding," and keep mind and heart at ease, free from burdensome care.

Prayer and Fasting
ANDREW MURRAY

Jesus said unto them. . . . Howbeit this kind goeth not out but by prayer and fasting.
MATTHEW 17:20–21

Jesus teaches us that a life of faith requires both prayer and fasting. Prayer grasps the power of heaven, fasting loosens the hold on earthly pleasure.

Jesus Himself fasted to get strength to resist the

devil. He taught His disciples that fasting should be in secret, and the Father would reward it openly. Abstinence from food, or moderation in taking it, helps to focus on communication with God.

Let's remember that abstinence, moderation, and self-denial are a help to the spiritual life. After having eaten a hearty meal, one does not feel much desire to pray. To willingly sacrifice our own pleasure or enjoyment will help to focus our minds more fully on God and His priorities. The very practice needed in overcoming our own desires will give us strength to take hold of God in prayer.

Our lack of discipline in prayer comes from our fleshly desire of comfort and ease. "And they that are Christ's have crucified the flesh with the affections and lusts" (Galatians 5:24). Prayer is not easy work. For the real practice of prayer—taking hold of God and having communion and fellowship with Him—it is necessary that our selfish desires be sacrificed.

Isn't it worth the trouble to deny ourselves daily in order to meet the holy God and receive His blessings?

Heart Ease
E. M. BOUNDS

Paul in writing to the Corinthians says, "I would have you without carefulness" (1 Corinthians 7:32), and this is the will of God. Prayer has the ability to do this very thing. "Casting all your care upon him; for he careth for you," is the way Peter puts it in 1 Peter 5:7; while Psalm 37:8 says, "Fret not thyself in any wise to do evil." Oh, the blessedness of a heart at ease from all inward care, exempt from undue anxiety, in the enjoyment of the peace of God which passeth all understanding!

The Sacrifice of a Worldly Heart
Andrew Murray

Then came the disciples to Jesus apart, and said, Why could not we cast him out? And Jesus said unto them, Because of your unbelief.
Matthew 17:19–20

The disciples had often cast out demons. But here they had been powerless. They asked the Lord what the reason might be. His answer is very simple: "Because of your unbelief."

How is it that we cannot live that life of unbroken fellowship with Christ which the Scripture promises? Simply because of our unbelief. We do not realize that faith must accept and expect that God will, by His almighty power, fulfill every promise He has made. We do not live in that utter helplessness and dependence on God alone which is the very essence of faith. We are not strong in the faith, fully persuaded that what God has promised He is able and willing to perform.

But what is the reason why this faith is so often lacking? "Howbeit this kind goeth not out but by prayer and fasting" [Matthew 17:21]. To have a strong faith in God requires a life in close touch with Him by persistent prayer. We cannot call up faith at our bidding; it needs close communion with God through prayer. It needs the denial of self—the sacrifice of a worldly heart. Just as we need God to give us faith and power, He, too, needs our whole being to be utterly given up to Him. Prayer and fasting are essential to this.

New Victory

JOHN WESLEY

Every new victory which a soul gains is the effect of a new prayer. . . . In the greatest temptations, a single look to Christ, and the barely pronouncing his name, suffices to overcome the wicked one, provided that it is done with confidence and calmness of spirit.

(IN WHAT WAY AND BY WHAT MEANS)

Now that you know the ins and outs of the who, what, when, where, and why about prayer, *how* do you *live* a life of prayer? Our four schoolmasters answer that question and more with the following prayer pointers, tips, insights, approaches, and more. Keeping in mind that knowledge is great but worthless unless what is learned is practiced, ask God, His Son, and the Holy Spirit to lead you to the method of prayer They would have you implement in your own life.

The "How" of God's Will

According to God's Will
ANDREW MURRAY

And this is the confidence that we have in him, that, if we ask any thing according to his will, he heareth us.
1 JOHN 5:14

How can we know if we are praying according to God's will? That is an intensely practical question to ask as we take time to pray.

To properly understand 1 John 5:14, we must connect the words "according to his will" with "ask"—not merely with "any thing." Similarly connect "he heareth" with "if we ask." Not only the thing asked for but also the disposition and character of the one asking must be in line with God's will. Both the thing asked for and the spirit of asking must be in harmony with God's will.

Jesus' teaching continually connected the answer to prayer with a life that was being lived according to God's will: trusting, forgiving, merciful, humble, believing, asking in His name, abiding in His love, observing/keeping His commands, and having His words abiding within. He also said that if they loved Him and kept His commands, then He would pray to the Father for them. Prayer has power according to the life! A life in line with God's will can ask according to God's will.

When you live according to God's will, you are spiritually able to discern what to ask for. A life yielded to and molded by the will of God will know what and how to pray. Boldness in prayer comes from the assurance that the spirit of asking and the thing asked are both according to the will of God.

Learning God's Will
S. D. GORDON

Learning His will here hinges upon three things: I must keep *in touch* with Him so He has an open ear to talk into. I must *delight* to do His will, *because it is His*. The third thing needs special emphasis. Many who are right on the first two stumble here: *His Word must be allowed to discipline my judgment as to Himself and His will*. Many of us stumble on number one and on number two, and a great many willing, earnest men sprawl badly when it comes to number three. The bother with these is the lack of a disciplined judgment about God and His will. If we would prayerfully *absorb* the Book, there would come a better poised judgment. We need to get a broad sweep of God's thought, to breathe Him in as He reveals Himself in this Book. The meek man—the man willing to yield his will to a higher will—will He guide in his judgment, that is, in his mental processes.

The Greatest Prayer

There is a greatest prayer that can be offered. It is the undercurrent in the stream of all Spirit-breathed prayer. Jesus Himself gives it to us in the only form of prayer He left for our use. It is small in size but mighty in power. Four words: "Thy will be done."

. . .Health, strength, home, loved ones, friendships, money, guidance, protecting care, the necessities, the extras that love ever thinks of, service—all these are included in God's loving thought for us. That is His will. It is modified by the degree of our consent, and further modified by the circumstances of our lives. Life has become a badly tangled skein of threads. With infinite patience and skill God is at work untangling and bringing the best possible out of the tangle. . . .

"Thy will be done" is the great dominant purpose-prayer that has been the pathway of God in all His great doings among men.

With this prayer go two clauses that explain it. . . .

The first clause is this: "Thy kingdom come." In both of these short sentences—"Thy will be done," "Thy kingdom come"—the emphatic word is *Thy*. That word is set in sharpest possible contrast here. There is another kingdom now on the earth. There is another will being done. This other kingdom must go if God's kingdom is to come. These kingdoms are antagonistic at every point of contact. They are rivals for the same allegiance and the same territory. They cannot exist together.

The second clause included in the prayer is this: "Deliver us from evil." These two sentences—"Thy will be done" and "deliver us from evil"—are naturally connected. Each statement includes the other. To have God's will fully done in us means emancipation from every influence of the evil one. To be delivered from the evil one means that every thought and plan of God for our lives will be fully carried out.

The Word of God as Guide
ANDREW MURRAY

For the word of God is quick, and powerful.
HEBREWS 4:12

I find it a great help to use God's Word in my prayers. If the Holy Spirit impresses a certain text upon my mind, I plead the promise. This habit increases our faith, reminds us of God's promises, and brings us into harmony with God's will. We learn to pray according to God's will and understand that we can only expect an answer when our prayers are in accordance with that will (1 John 5:14).

Prayer is like fire. Fire can only burn brightly if it is supplied with good fuel. That fuel is God's Word which must be studied carefully and prayerfully. His Word must be taken into the heart and lived out in the life.

We are all familiar with the characteristics of a seed—a small grain in which the life-power of a whole tree slumbers. If it is placed in the soil, it will grow and increase and become a large tree. Each word or promise of God is a seed containing a divine life in it. If I carry it in my heart by faith, love it, and meditate on it, it will slowly, surely spring up and bring forth the fruit of righteousness.

The Holy Spirit uses both the Word and prayer. Prayer is the expression of our human need and desire. The Holy Spirit teaches us to use the Word as a guide to what God will do for us.

Contrary to the Love of God
JOHN WESLEY

As many as I love, I rebuke. . . . Be zealous therefore, and repent.
REVELATION 3:19

Sooner or later after he is justified, the believer feels *self-will*, a will contrary to the will of God. Now a *will* is an essential part of the nature of every intelligent being, even of our blessed Lord Himself. But His human will was always subject to the will of His Father.

The case with even true believers in Christ is that they frequently find their will more or less exalting itself against the will of God. They fight against this self-will with all their might, and thus they continue in the faith.

But self-will, as well as pride, is a species of *idolatry*. Both are directly contrary to the love of God, as is *the love of the world*. It is true, when one first passes from death unto life, he desires nothing more but God. He can truly say, "There is none upon earth that I desire beside You!"

But it is not always so. If he does not continually watch and pray, he feels not only the love of the world but also *lust* reviving and the assaults of *inordinate affection*. He feels the strongest urges toward loving the creature more than the Creator—be it a child, a parent, a husband, a wife, or a well-beloved friend. To the extent he yields to the desire of earthly things or pleasures, he is prone to forget God. And for this, even the true believer in Christ needs to repent.

Yielded

ANDREW MURRAY

Ye have need of patience, that, after ye have done the will of God, ye might receive the promise.
HEBREWS 10:36

The first concern of most Christians in trouble is to be delivered from it. However, perhaps this should not be the primary thing. Our one great desire ought to be that we do not fail in knowing or doing the will of God in anything. This is the secret of strength and true character in the Christian life.

When trials come, though, it is beyond human power to think of and do God's will first. It is indeed something beyond human power but not beyond the power of grace. It is just for this that our Lord Jesus came to earth—to do God's will. He went to the cross with the prayer to God: "Not my will, but thine, be done" [Luke 22:42].

Ask God to renew your spirit and your mind and to show you how He would have you live wholly in His will. Yield yourself to that will in everything you know, and do it. Yield yourself to that will in all its divine love and quickening power as it works in you and makes you partaker of its inmost nature. Pray,

pray, pray, until you see increasingly in Jesus' life and death the promise and pledge of what God will work in you. Your abiding in Him and your oneness with Him mean nothing less than your being called to do the will of God as He did it.

Full Deliverance
E. M. BOUNDS

Paul's injunction which includes both God's promise and His purpose, and which immediately precedes his entreaty to be "careful for nothing" [Philippians 4:6] reads on this wise: "Rejoice in the Lord always, and again I say, Rejoice. Let your moderation be made known to all men. The Lord is at hand" (Philippians 4:4–5).

In a world filled with cares of every kind, where temptation is the rule, where there are so many things to try us, how is it possible to rejoice always? We look at the naked, dry command, and we accept it and reverence it as the Word of God, but no joy comes. How are we to let our moderation, our mildness, and our gentleness be universally and always known? We resolve to be benign and gentle. We remember the nearness of the Lord, but still we are hasty, quick, hard, and salty. We listen to the divine charge, "Be careful for nothing," yet still we are anxious, care-worn, care-eaten, and care-tossed. How can we fulfill the divine word, so sweet and so large in promise, so beautiful in the eye, and yet so far from being real-ized? How can we enter upon the rich patrimony of being true, honest, just, and pure, and possess lovely things? The recipe is infallible, the remedy is univer-sal, and the cure is unfailing. It is found in the words which we have so often herein referred to of Paul: "Be careful for nothing; but in every thing by prayer and supplication with thanksgiving let your requests be made known unto God" (Philippians 4:6).

This joyous, carefree, peaceful experience bringing the believer into a joyousness, living simply by faith day by day, is the will of God. Writing in 1 Thessalonians 5:16–18, Paul tells them: "Rejoice evermore. Pray without ceasing. In every thing give thanks: for this is the will of God in Christ Jesus concerning you." So that not only is it God's will that we should find full deliverance from all care and undue anxiety, but He has ordained prayer as the means by which we can reach that happy state of heart.

The One Purpose of Prayer
S. D. GORDON

The greatest prayer anyone can offer is "Your will be done." It will be offered in a thousand different forms, with a thousand details, as needs arise daily. But every true prayer comes under those four words. There is not a good, desirable thing that you have thought of that He has not thought of first, and probably with an added touch not in your thoughts. . . .

It may help us here to remember that God has a first and a second will for us: a first choice and a second. He always prefers that His first will be accomplished in us. But where we will not be wooed up to that height, He comes down to the highest level we will come up to and works with us there.

God's Revealed Will

ANDREW MURRAY

[I pray] that he would grant you. . .to be strengthened with
might by his Spirit in the inner man.
EPHESIANS 3:16

Pray for the full manifestation of the grace and energy of the Holy Spirit to remove all that is contrary to God's revealed will. Do this so that we do not grieve the Holy Spirit. Then He can work with mightier power in the Church for the exaltation of Christ and for our blessing.

All prayer unites in the one request—the power of the Holy Spirit. Make it your prayer.

Pray as a child asks a father. "If a son shall ask bread of any of you that is a father, will he give him a stone? . . . If ye then, being evil, know how to give good gifts unto your children: how much more shall your heavenly Father give the Holy Spirit to them that ask him?" (Luke 11:11, 13).

Ask as simply and trustfully as a child asks for food. You can do this because "God hath sent forth the Spirit of his Son into your hearts, crying, Abba, Father" (Galatians 4:6). This Spirit is in you to give you child-like confidence. Have faith in the fact that He is praying in you. In that faith ask for the power of the Holy Spirit everywhere. Mention places or groups where you especially desire it to be seen.

The Spirit's Prayer Room

S. D. GORDON

The great truth is that the Spirit within us prays God's

will. He teaches us God's will, He teaches us how to pray God's will, and He Himself prays God's will in us. Further, He seeks to pray God's will in us before we have yet reached up to where we know ourselves what that will is.

We should be ambitious to cultivate a healthy sensitivity to this indwelling Spirit. And when there comes that quick inner wooing to pray, let us faithfully obey. Even though we are not clear what the particular petition is to be, let us remain in prayer while He uses us as the conduit of His praying.

Often the best prayer to offer about some friend or some particular thing after perhaps stating the case the best we can is this: "Holy Spirit, be praying in me the thing the Father wants done. Father, what the Spirit within me is praying, that is my prayer in Jesus' name. Your will, what You are wishing and thinking, may that be fully done here."

A Prayer
JOHN WESLEY

Lord, I am no longer my own, but Yours.
Put me to what You will,
rank me with whom You will.
Let me be employed by You
or laid aside for You,
exalted for You or brought low by You.
Let me have all things,
let me have nothing,
I freely and heartily yield all things
to Your pleasure and disposal.
And now, O glorious and blessed God,

Father, Son, and Holy Spirit,
You are mine and I am Yours.
So be it. Amen.

The "How" of Relationship

Close with Christ
ANDREW MURRAY

I have been purchased with the blood of Christ. I am to live every day with one thought, "How can I please my Master?"

We find the Christian life so difficult because we seek for God's blessing while we live life according to our own desires. We make our own plans and choose our own work. Then we ask the Lord to help us not to go too far wrong. Instead, our relationship with Jesus should be that we are entirely at His disposal. We should ask Him daily, "Lord, is there anything in me that is not according to Your will, that is not entirely surrendered to You?"

If we will wait patiently for His guidance there will spring up a relationship between us and Christ so close that we will be amazed. He will take actual possession of us and give us unbroken fellowship.

Right Relationship with God
S. D. GORDON

Now there are the same two hows in praying. First the relationship must be established before any business can be transacted. Then skill must be acquired in the transacting of the business at hand.

Right now let's talk about the first of these, the how of relationship in prayer. The basis of prayer is right relationship with God. Prayer is representing God in the spirit realm of this world. It is insisting upon His rights down in this sphere of action. It is standing for Him with full powers from Him. Clearly the only basis of such relationship to God is *Jesus*. We have been outlawed by sin. We were in touch with God. We broke with Him. The break could not be repaired by us. Jesus came. He was God *and* Man. He touches both. We get back only through Him. The blood of the cross is the basis of all prayer. Through it the relationship is established that underlies all prayer. Only as I come to God through Jesus to get the sin score straightened, and only as I keep in sympathy with Jesus in the purpose of my life, can I practice prayer.

Continual Relationship
ANDREW MURRAY

Be careful for nothing; but in every thing by prayer and supplication with thanksgiving let your requests be made known unto God.
PHILIPPIANS 4:6

Seeing and knowing our selfish condition calls us to prayer. The desire of our heart becomes the spirit of prayer. What characteristics of prayer should distinguish the Christian?

At times an honest person may show honesty by actions. At other times there is no special situation to confirm this honesty. But honesty is, all the same, the inward living principle of that person's heart. Just so the spirit of prayer may quietly possess the heart without interruption and at other times may have certain hours of prayer. But prayer that has its own life and spirit is vastly superior to any ritual form. It is independent and has no particular hours or forms of work.

It would be worthwhile to study the place that the word *continual* ought to have in our life: continual joy of the infinite love of God towards us; continual unalterable dependence upon God every hour of our life; the continual receiving of goodness and happiness from God alone; the continual denial of our evil nature; the continual and immediate inspiration of the Holy Spirit maintaining the life of Christ in us; the continual breathing of the heart after God in prayer; and then the continual loving Him with our whole heart.

Man's Part, God's Part
E. M. BOUNDS

Think about God. Make much of Him, till He broadens and fills the horizon of your faith. Then prayer will come into its marvelous inheritance of wonders. The marvels of prayer are seen when we remember that God's purposes are changed by prayer, God's vengeance is stayed by prayer, and God's penalty is remitted by prayer. The whole range of God's dealing with man is affected by prayer. Here is a force which must be increasingly used, that of prayer, a force to which all the events of life ought to be subjected.

To "pray without ceasing," to pray in everything, and to pray everywhere—these commands of continuity are expressive of the sleepless energy of prayer, of the exhaustless possibilities of prayer, and of its exacting necessity. Prayer can do all things. Prayer must do all things.

Prayer is asking God for something, and for something which He has promised. Prayer is using the divinely appointed means for obtaining what we need and for accomplishing what God proposes to do on earth.

Prayer is appointed to convey
the blessings God designs to give;
Long as they live should Christians pray,
they learn to pray when first they live.

And prayer brings to us blessings which we need, and which only God can give, and which prayer can alone convey to us.

In their broadest fullness, the possibilities of prayer are to be found in the very nature of prayer. This service of prayer is not a mere rite, a ceremony through which we go, a sort of performance. Prayer is going to God for something needed and desired. Prayer is simply asking God to do for us what He has promised us He will do if we ask Him. The answer is a part of prayer and is God's part of it. God's doing the thing asked for is as much a part of the prayer as the asking of the thing is prayer. Asking is man's part. Giving is God's part. The praying belongs to us. The answer belongs to God.

Wholehearted Seeking of the Spirit
Andrew Murray

Ye shall seek me, and find me, when ye shall search for me
with all your heart.
Jeremiah 29:13

It's often been said that if one seeks to perform any great work, he must do it with his whole heart and with all his might. In business this is the secret of success. Above all in spiritual things it is indispensable, especially in praying for the Holy Spirit.

Let me repeat that the Holy Spirit desires to have full possession of you. He can be satisfied with nothing less if He is to show His full power in your life.

Do you realize when you pray for the Holy Spirit that you are praying for the whole Godhead to take possession of you? Have your prayers had a wrong motive? If you were expecting that God would do something in your heart but in other things you would be free to do your own will, that would be a great mistake. The Holy Spirit must have full possession.

You may not feel a burning, urgent desire for the Holy Spirit to have full control, and you do not see any chance of its becoming true in your life. God knows about this inability of yours; He has ordained that the Holy Spirit will work within you all you need. What God demands of us, He will work within us. On our part there must be earnest prayer each day and an acceptance of the Holy Spirit as our leader.

Child of God, the Holy Spirit longs to possess you wholly. Submit yourself in complete dependence on His promise.

The "How" of Method

A Good Plan
ANDREW MURRAY

Be careful for nothing; but in every thing by prayer and

supplication with thanksgiving let your requests be made
known unto God.
PHILIPPIANS 4:6

Whenever we come in prayer to present our requests to God, our Lord instructs us to pause long enough to remember who He is: our King, our Righteousness. His Word tells us of His kingdom—the realm in which His servants' requests are to be made.

If we don't acknowledge who He is, prayer is not prayer at all. Instead, the recitation of our worries is simply an attempt to worry God. God is already aware of our needs. He wants us to think over what we ask from Him. Do not be satisfied with going over the same things every day. No child goes on saying the same thing day after day to his earthly father.

Conversation with the Father is colored by the needs of the day. Let your prayer be something definite, rising out of the Word which you have read or out of the real soul—needs which you long to have satisfied. Let your prayer be so definite that you can say, "I know what I have asked for from my Father, and I expect an answer."

It is a good plan sometimes to take a piece of paper and write down what you pray for. You might keep such a paper for a week or more and repeat the prayers until some new need arises.

Purpose-full Prayer
S. D. GORDON

The first thing in prayer is to find God's purpose; the second thing is to make that purpose our prayer. We want to find out what God is thinking and then claim that which will be done....

Now prayer is this: finding out God's purpose for our lives and for the earth and insisting that that will be done here. The great thing then is to find out and insist on God's will. And the "how" of method in prayer is concerned with that....

Sometimes I feel clear about the particular prayer to offer, but many times I am puzzled to know. I may not know *all* the facts. I know this man who evidently needs prayer, a Christian man perhaps, but there may be some fact in there I do not know that seriously affects the whole difficulty. And I am compelled to fall back on this: I don't know how to pray as I ought, but the Spirit within me will make intercession for this man as I allow Him to have full sway in me as the conduit of His prayer. And He who is listening above as He hears His will for this man being repeated down on the battlefield will recognize His own purpose, and so that thing will be working out because of Jesus' victory over the evil one.

Definite Requests
Andrew Murray

Pray with definite requests. Jesus asked the blind beggar, "What wilt thou that I shall do unto thee?" (Luke 18:41). The Lord knew what the man wanted, and yet He asked him. Verbalizing our wish gives meaning to our transaction with God. It awakens faith and expectation.

Being definite in your requests also helps you to know what answer you are looking for. Ask those you are praying for what they need. If they have prayer letters, use them as guides. Intercession is not mere words and pious wishes. Its aim is to receive and bring down blessing through believing, persevering prayer.

Six Suggestions on How to Pray
S. D. GORDON

There are six suggestions here on how to pray. First, we need time for prayer, unhurried, daily time. . . .

The second suggestion: We need a place for prayer.

The third suggestion needs much emphasis today: Give the Book of God its place in prayer. Prayer is not talking to God—simply. It is listening first, then talking.

The fourth suggestion is this: Let the Spirit teach you how to pray. . . . .

When you go alone in the quiet time and place with the Book, quietly pray: "Blessed Prayer Spirit, teach me how to pray," and He will. Do not be nervous, wondering if you will understand. Study to be quiet. Be still and listen.

You will find your praying changing. You will talk more simply. You will quit asking for some things. Some of the old forms of prayer will likely drop from your lips. You will use fewer words maybe, but they will be spoken with a quiet, absolute faith that this thing you are asking is being worked out.

This thing of letting the Spirit teach must come first in one's praying, remain to the last, and continue all along as the leading dominant factor. The highest law of the Christian life is obedience to the leading of the Holy Spirit. There needs to be a cultivated judgment in reading His leading and not mistaking our haphazard thoughts as His voice. He should be allowed to teach us how to pray, and more—to dominate our praying . . . . So there needs to be special seasons of persistent prayer, a continuing until victory is assured. Obey His promptings. Sometimes there comes an impulse to pray or to ask another to pray. And we think, *I have just been praying*, or *he prays about this anyway. It is not necessary to pray again. I do not want to suggest it*. Better obey the impulse quietly, with few words of explanation to the other one concerned, or no words beyond simply the request.

You will notice that the chief purpose of these four suggestions is to learn God's will. The quiet place, the quiet time, the Book, the Spirit—this is the schoolroom. Here we learn His will. Learning that makes one eager to have it done and breathes new life into the longing prayer that it may be done.

There is a fine word much used in the Psalms and in Isaiah for this sort of thing—*waiting*. Over and over again that is the word used for the contact with God that reveals to us His will and imparts to us anew His desires. It is a word full of richest and deepest meaning. Waiting is not an occasional or hurried thing. It means *steadfastness*, that is holding on; *patience*, that is holding back; *expectancy*, that is holding the face up to see; *obedience*, that is holding one's self in readiness to go or do; *listening*, that is holding quiet and still so as to hear.

The fifth suggestion. . . . Prayer must be *in Jesus' name*. The relationship of prayer is through Jesus. And the prayer itself must be offered in His name, because the whole strength of the case lies in Jesus. Let us distinctly bear in mind that we have no standing with God except through Jesus.

The sixth suggestion is a familiar one, and yet one much misunderstood. Prayer must be *in faith*. But please note that faith here is not believing that God *can* but that He *will*. It is kneeling and making the prayer and then saying, "Father, I thank You for this; that it will be so, I thank You." Then rising and going about your duties, saying, "That thing is settled." Repeating the prayer with the thanks, and then saying as you go off, "That matter is assured." Not going repeatedly to persuade God but understanding that prayer is the deciding factor in a spirit conflict and each prayer is like a fresh blow between the eyes of the enemy. . . .

That faith has four simple characteristics. It is intelligent. It finds out what God's will is. Faith is never contrary to reason. Sometimes it is a bit higher up; the reasoning process has not yet reached it. Second, it is obedient. It fits its life into God's will. There is apt to be a stiff rub here all the time. Then it is expectant. It looks out for the result. It bows down upon the earth but sends a man to keep an eye on the sea [see 1 Kings 18:43]. And then it is persistent. It hangs on. It says, "Go again seven times, seventy times seven." It reasons that having learned God's will and knowing that He does not change, the delay must be caused by the third person, the enemy, and that stubborn persistence in the Victor's name routs him and leaves a clear field.

Take Hold and Stir Up

ANDREW MURRAY

Let him take hold of my strength, that he may make peace with me.
ISAIAH 27:5

There is none that calleth upon thy name, that stirreth up himself to take hold of thee.
ISAIAH 64:7

Stir up the gift of God, which is in thee.
2 TIMOTHY 1:6

First, take hold of God's strength. God is a Spirit. I cannot take hold of Him and hold Him fast but by the Spirit. Take hold of God's strength, and hold on 'til it has done for you what He has promised. Pray for the power of the Spirit to convict of sin.

Second, stir up yourself, the power that is in you by the Holy Spirit, to take hold. Give your whole heart and will to it, and say, "I will not let Thee go except Thou bless me."

Take Time to Worship
ANDREW MURRAY

Ye believe in God, believe also in me.
JOHN 14:1

When Christ was about to leave His disciples, He taught them that they were to believe in Him with the same perfect confidence with which they had believed in God. "Believe me that I am in the Father. . . . He that believeth on me, the works that I do shall he do also" (John 14:11–12). Here on earth He had not been able to make Himself fully known to His disciples. But in heaven, the fullness of God's power would be His. Jesus would do greater things in and through His disciples than He had ever done here on earth.

This faith must focus itself on the person of Christ in His union with the Father. The disciples were to have perfect confidence that all God had done could now be done by Jesus, too. The deity of Christ is the rock on which our faith depends. God's power has worked in Christ through His resurrection from the dead. Christ can also, in His divine power, work in us all that we need.

Take time in prayer to worship Jesus in His divine omnipotence as one with the Father. Bow in deep humility before the Lord Jesus and worship Him as Thomas did: "My LORD and my God!" (John 20:28). Let the Savior you have known and loved become, as never before, the Mighty God. Let Him always be your confidence and your strength.

Man's Wholehearted Prayer
ANDREW MURRAY

The LORD. . .grant thee according to thine own heart.
PSALM 20:1, 4

Thou hast given him his heart's desire.
PSALM 21:2

I cried with my whole heart; hear me, O LORD.
PSALM 119:145

God lives and listens to every petition with His whole heart. Each time we pray, the whole infinite God is there to hear. He asks that in each prayer the whole man shall be there, too; that we shall cry with our whole heart. Christ gave Himself to God for men; and so He takes up every need into His intercession. If once we seek God with our whole heart, the whole heart will be in every prayer with which we come to this God. Pray with your whole heart for the young.

Take Time to Understand
ANDREW MURRAY

What is it then? I will pray with the spirit, and I will pray with the understanding.
1 CORINTHIANS 14:15

We need to pray with the spirit, as the vehicle of the intercession of God's Spirit, if we are to take hold of God in faith and power. We need to pray with the understanding, if we are really to enter deeply into the needs we bring before Him. Take time to apprehend intelligently, in each subject, the nature, the extent, the urgency of the request, the ground and way and certainty of God's promise as revealed in His Word. Let the mind affect the heart. Pray with the understanding and with the spirit.

Becoming Educated
ANDREW MURRAY

I exhort. . . supplications, prayers, intercessions, and giving of thanks, be made for all men.
1 TIMOTHY 2:1

Pray without ceasing. How can we learn to do that? The best way of learning to do a thing—in fact the only way—is to do it. Begin by setting apart some time every day, say ten or fifteen minutes, in which you say to God and to yourself that you come to Him now as intercessor for others. It can be in the morning, in the evening, or any other time. Do not worry if you cannot set aside the same time every day. Just see that you do it. Christ chose you and appointed you to pray for others.

If at first you do not feel any special urgency, faith, or power in your prayers, do not let that hinder you. Quietly tell the Lord Jesus of your weakness. Believe that the Holy Spirit is in you to teach you to pray. Be assured that, if you begin, God will help you. God cannot help you unless you begin and keep on.

Pray at all times. How do I know what to pray for? Once you begin to think of all the needs around you, you will soon find enough to pray for. But to help you, each day for the next few weeks we will concentrate on subjects and hints for prayer. Use and reuse these ideas until you know more fully to follow the Spirit's leading and have learned, if need be, to make your own list of subjects. These days can be a time of becoming educated in this matter of praying at all times.

The "Flow" of Approach

With Meekness
ANDREW MURRAY

Come unto me, all ye that labour and are heavy laden, and I will give you rest.
MATTHEW 11:28

When Jesus was on earth He did not mention meekness as one of several other virtues that were to be learned from Him, but rather as the one which was His primary characteristic—the one which we must learn if we are to find rest for our souls. He came to deliver us from the sins of self-exaltation and pride.

In heaven He humbled Himself as Son before the

Father, that He might be sent as a servant into the world. He humbled Himself to become man. As man He humbled Himself to the death of the cross. He had to come into the world as the gentle Lamb of God to bring to earth the meekness of heart in which true submission to God is manifested.

There is no way to heaven except by meekness, by entirely dying to our pride, and by living entirely in the lowliness of Jesus. Pride gives no rest; it is from hell. It must die or nothing of heaven can live in us. As we come to Him in prayer, God will certainly bestow this meekness and by His Spirit work it out in the heart of everyone who surrenders his life entirely to the power of the blood of the Lamb.

The Spirit works as the Spirit of the Lamb. He works with a hidden but perfect power, breathing into the heart of His own people that which is the divine glory of the Lamb—His meekness.

With Obedience
ANDREW MURRAY

If ye abide in me, and my words abide in you, ye shall ask what ye will, and it shall be done unto you. . . . If ye keep my commandments, ye shall abide in my love.
JOHN 15:7, 10

If you make the morning hour holy to the Lord, the day with its duties will also be holy.

Do not forget the close bond between the inner chamber and the outer world. The attitude of prayer must remain with us all day. The object of the prayer is to so unite us with God that we may have Him always abiding with us.

Sin, thoughtlessness, and yielding to the flesh or to the world make us unfit for communion with God and bring a cloud over the soul. If you have stumbled or fallen, return to God in prayer. First invoke the blood of Jesus and claim cleansing by it. Do not rest till by confession you have repented of and put away your sin. Let the precious blood really give you a fresh freedom of approach to God.

Remember that the roots of your life in the inner chamber strike far out in body and soul so as to manifest themselves in daily life. Let the obedience of faith, in which you pray in secret, rule you constantly.

The inner chamber is intended to bind us to God, to supply us with power from God, to enable us to live for God alone. Thank God for the inner chamber and for the life which He will enable us to experience and nourish there.

With Open Ears and Heart
ANDREW MURRAY

Thus saith the LORD. . . . To this man will I look, even to him that is poor and of a contrite spirit, and trembleth at my word.
ISAIAH 66:1–2

Many of us are so occupied with how much or how little we have to say in our prayers that the voice of One speaking is never heard because it is not expected or waited for. We need to get into the right frame of mind and have a listening attitude.

In regard to the connection between prayer and the Word of God in our private devotion, this expression has often been quoted: "I pray, I speak to God; I read the Bible, God speaks to me." We need to ask how our Scripture reading and praying can become true fellowship with God.

A prayerful spirit is the spirit to which God will speak. Prayer prepares the heart for receiving the Word from God Himself, for the teaching of the Spirit to give the spiritual understanding of it, for the faith that is made part of its mighty working.

In God's Word we read what God will do in me, how God would have me come to Him in prayer, assurance that I will be heard, and what God will do in the world. A prayerful spirit will be a listening spirit waiting to hear what God says. In true communion with God, His presence and the part He takes must be as real as my own.

Let us prepare ourselves to pray with a heart that humbly waits to hear God speak. The greatest blessing in prayer will be our ceasing to pray to let God speak.

With Trust
ANDREW MURRAY

Truth, Lord: yet the dogs eat of the crumbs. . . . O woman, great is thy faith: be it unto thee even as thou wilt.
MATTHEW 15:27–28

You feel unworthy and unable to pray aright. To accept this heartily, and to be content still to come and be blessed in your unworthiness, is true humility. It proves its integrity by not seeking for anything, but simply trusting His grace. And so it is the very strength of a great faith that gets a full answer. "Yet the dogs"—let that be your plea as you persevere for someone possibly possessed of the devil. Let not your littleness hinder you for a moment.

With Humility

Andrew Murray

God resisteth the proud, but giveth grace unto the humble.
James 4:6

There is an infallible touchstone that will teach you the spirit of prayer. Pull away from the world and all activities. Stop the former workings of your heart and mind. With all your strength, spend all this month as continually as you can in one kind of prayer to God. Offer it frequently on your knees but, whether sitting, standing, or walking, always be inwardly longing and earnestly praying this one prayer to God.

Pray that He would show you and take from your heart every form of pride. Pray that He would awaken in you the depths of humility so that you will be open to His light and His Holy Spirit. Reject every thought except that of praying in this matter from the bottom of your heart.

The painful sense and feeling of what you are, kindled by the light of God within you, is the fire and light from which your spirit of prayer proceeds. At first nothing is found or felt but pain and darkness. But as this prayer of humility is met by the divine love, the mercy of God embraces it. Then your prayer is changed into songs and thanksgiving.

With a Cultivated "Attitude"

Andrew Murray

Pray one for another.
James 5:16

There is value in intercession. It is an indispensable part

of prayer. It strengthens our love and faith in what God can do, and it brings blessing and salvation to others. Prayer should be mainly for others, not for ourselves alone. Begin by praying for those near and dear to us, those with whom we live, that we may be of help to them and not a hindrance.

Pray for your friends and all with whom you come into contact. Pray for all Christians, especially for ministers and those in responsible positions.

Pray for those who do not yet know the Lord as their Savior. Make a list of the names of those God has laid upon your heart and pray for their conversion. Christ needs you to bring to Him in prayer the souls of those around you. Pray, too, for all poor and neglected ones. Pray for mission work. Use a mission calendar with daily subjects of prayer.

Do you think this will take too much time? Just think what an inconceivable blessing it is to help others through your prayers. Look to the Holy Spirit for further guidance. If morning is not the best time for you, schedule another time later in the day. Cultivate the attitude: "I am saved to serve."

With Quietness
ANDREW MURRAY

My soul waiteth upon God: from him cometh my salvation.
PSALM 62:1

Prayer has its power in God alone. The nearer a man comes to God Himself, the deeper he enters into God's will; the more he takes hold of God, the more power in prayer.

God must reveal Himself. If it please Him to make

Himself known, He can make the heart conscious of His presence. Our posture must be that of holy reverence, of quiet waiting and adoration. . . .

Be still before God. Thus you will get power to pray.

With God's Grace and Courage
ANDREW MURRAY

Who is sufficient for real intercession? The more we study and try to practice the grace of intercession, the more we feel overwhelmed by its greatness and our weakness. Let that feeling lead you to hear: "My grace is sufficient for thee," and to answer truthfully, "our sufficiency is of God" (2 Corinthians 12:9; 3:5).

Take courage; you are called to take part in the intercession of Christ. The burden and the agony, the triumph and the victory, are all His. Learn from Him; to know how to pray, yield to His Spirit in you. He gave Himself as a sacrifice to God for us that He might have the right and power of intercession. "He bare the sin of many, and made intercession for the transgressors" (Isaiah 53:12).

Let your faith rest boldly on His finished work. Let your heart identify with Him in His death and His life. Like Him, give yourself to God as a sacrifice for others. It is your highest calling, your true and full union with Him.

Come and give your whole heart and life to intercession, and you will know its blessedness and its power. God asks nothing less; the world needs nothing less; Christ asks nothing less; let nothing less be what we offer to God.

With Boldness
ANDREW MURRAY

Pray boldly. "We have a great High Priest. . .Jesus the Son of God. . . . Let us therefore come boldly unto the throne of grace" (Hebrews 4:14, 16).

As we have been thinking about the work of intercession, what is it doing for us? Does it make us aware of our weakness in prayer? Thank God for this. It is the very first lesson we need on the way to praying the "effectual fervent prayer of a righteous man availeth much" (James 5:16). Let us persevere taking each item boldly to the throne of grace.

As we pray, we shall learn to pray, to believe, and to expect with increasing boldness. Hold fast your confidence; it is at God's command you come as an intercessor. Christ will give you grace to pray as you should.

The "How" of Listening

Eyes and Ears
S. D. GORDON

The beginning of that long eighteenth chapter of 1 Kings that tells of the Carmel conflict begins with a message to Elijah from God: "The word of the LORD came to Elijah. . .I will send rain upon the earth" [verse 1]. That was the foundation of that persistent praying and sevenfold watching on the mountaintop. First the ear heard, then the voice persistently claimed, then the eye expectantly looked. First the voice of God, then the voice of man. That is the true order. Tremendous results always follow that combination. . . .

With us the training is of the *inner* ear. And its first training, after the early childhood stage is passed, must usually be through the eye. What God has spoken to others has been written down for us. We hear through our eyes. The eye opens the way to the inner ear. God spoke in His Word. He is still speaking in it and through it. The whole thought here is to get *to know God*. He reveals Himself in the word that comes from His own lips and through His messengers' lips. He reveals Himself in His dealings with men. Every incident and experience of these pages is a mirror held up to God's face. In them we may come to see Him.

This is studying the Bible not for the Bible's sake but for the purpose of knowing God. The object aimed at is not the Book but the God revealed in the Book.

A Spirit-Illumined Mind

S. D. GORDON

I want to make some simple suggestions for studying this Book so as to get to God through it. First there must be the *time* element. One must get at least a half hour daily when the mind is fresh. A tired mind does not readily *absorb*. This should be persisted in until there is a habitual spending of at least that much time daily over the Book, with a spirit at leisure from all else so it can take in. Then the time should be given to *the Book itself*. If other books are consulted and read, let that be *after* the reading of this Book. Let God talk to you directly, rather than through somebody else. Give Him first chance at your ears. This Book in the central place of your table, the others grouped about it.

A third suggestion brings out the circle of this work. *Read prayerfully.* We learn how to pray by reading prayerfully. This Book does not reveal its sweetness and strength to the sharp mind merely but to the Spirit-enlightened mind.

There is a fourth word to put in here. We must read *thoughtfully.* Fight shallowness. Insist on reading thoughtfully. A word in the Bible for this is *meditate.* Run through and pick out this word with its variations. The word underneath that English word means "to mutter," as though a man were repeating something over and over again as he turned it over in his mind. We have another word with the same meaning that is not used much now—*ruminate.* We call the cow a ruminant because she chews the cud. She will spend hours chewing the cud and then give us the rich milk that she has extracted from her food. That is the word here—*ruminate.* Chew the cud if you want to get the richest cream and butter.

There is a fifth suggestion that is easier to make than to follow. *Read obediently.* As the truth appeals to your conscience, *let it change your habit and life.*

Then one needs to have a *plan* of reading. A consecutive plan gathers up the fragments of time into a strong whole. Get a good plan and stick to it. Better a fairly good plan faithfully followed than the best plan if used only occasionally. . . .

I want to especially urge *wide reading* as being the basis of all study. It is the simple, the natural, the scientific method. It is adapted to all classes of persons. It is *the* method of all for all. It underlies all methods of getting a grasp of this wonderful Book and so coming to as full an understanding of God as is possible.

By wide reading is meant a *rapid reading through* regardless of verse, chapter, or book divisions. Reading it as *a narrative*, a story, as you would read any book. There will be a reverence of spirit with this book that no other inspires, but with the same intellectual method of running through to see what is here. No book is so fascinating as the Bible when read this way.

To illustrate, begin at Genesis and read rapidly through *by the page*. Do not try to understand all. You won't. Just push on. Do not try to remember everything. Do not think about that. Let stick to you what will. You will be surprised to find how much will. You may read ten or twelve pages in your first half hour. Next time start in where you left off. You may get through Genesis in three or four sessions, more or less, depending on your mood and how fast your habit of reading may be.

But do not stop at the close of Genesis. Push on into Exodus. The connection is immediate. It is the same book. And so on into Leviticus. Now do not try to understand Leviticus the first time, but you can easily group its contents into the offerings, the law of offerings, incidents, and sanitary regulations. And in it all you will be getting the picture of God—*that is the point*. And so on through the Bible.

A second stage of this wide reading is fitting together the parts. The arrangement of our Bible is not chronological but topical. For example, open your Bible to the close of Esther and again at the close of Malachi. The books from Genesis to Esther we know as the historical section, and this second section the poetical and prophetical section. There is some history in the prophecy, and some prophecy and poetry in the historical part, but in the main the first part is historical and the second poetry and prophecy. These two parts belong together. Fit the poetry and the prophecy into the history. Do it on your own, as though it had never been done. It has been done much better than you will do it, and you will make some mistakes. You can check them afterward in some scholarly books. You cannot tell where some parts belong, but meanwhile the thing to note is this: You are absorbing the Book. It is becoming a part of you. There is coming a new vision of God, which will radically transform the reverent student. In it all seek to acquire *the historical sense.* That is, step back and see what this thing or that meant to these men as it was first spoken under their immediate circumstances.

And so push on into the New Testament. Do not try so much to fit the four Gospels into one connected story, dovetailing all the parts, but try rather to get a clear grasp of Jesus' movements those few years as told by these four men. Fit Paul's letters into the book of Acts the best you can.

You see at once that this is a method not for a month, nor for a year, but for years. The topical and textual study grow naturally out of it. And meanwhile you are getting an intelligent grasp of this wondrous classic, you are absorbing the finest literature in the English tongue, and infinitely better yet, you are breathing into your very being a new, deep, broad, tender conception of *God.*

Silent Listening Before God
ANDREW MURRAY

For ye are the temple of the living God.
2 CORINTHIANS 6:16

After worshiping God in prayer with praise and thanksgiving, prepare yourself for intercessory prayer by waiting on God in meditative, prayerful Bible study.

One reason why the discipline of prayer is not attractive is that people do not know how to pray. Their stock of words is soon exhausted, and they do not know what else to say. This happens because they forget that prayer is not a soliloquy where everything comes from one side, but it is a dialogue where God's child listens to what the Father says, replies to it, and then asks for the things he needs.

Read a few verses from the Bible. Do not concern yourself with the difficult parts in them; you can consider these later. Take what you understand, apply it to yourself, and ask the Father to make His Word light and power in your heart. Thus you will have material enough for prayer from the Word which the Father speaks to you. You will also have the liberty to ask for things you need.

Keep on in this way, and prayer will become at length, not a place where you sigh and struggle, but a place of living fellowship with the Father in heaven. Prayerful study of the Bible is indispensable for powerful prayer. The Word prayerfully read and cherished in the heart by faith will, through the Spirit, be both light and life within us.

The Only Refuge for Love
ANDREW MURRAY

Trouble me not: the door is now shut, and my children are with me in bed; I cannot rise and give thee.
LUKE 11:7

We often speak of the power of love. In one sense this is true, and yet the truth has limitations. The strongest love may be utterly inadequate. A mother might be willing to give her life for her dying child but still not be able to save it. The host at midnight was most willing to give his friend bread, but he had none. It was this sense of inadequacy that sent him begging, "A friend of mine. . .is come to me, and I have nothing to set before him." This sense of inadequacy gives strength to the life of intercession.

"I have nothing to set before him." As we are aware of our inadequacies, intercession becomes the only hope and refuge. I may have knowledge, a loving heart, and be ready to give myself for those under my charge, but I cannot give them the bread of heaven. With all my love and zeal, still "I have nothing to set before them."

Blessed are you if you have made "I have nothing" the motto of your ministry. You think of the judgment day and the danger of those without Christ and recognize a supernatural power is needed to save people from sin. You feel utterly insufficient—all you can do is to meet their natural need. "I have nothing" motivates you to pray. Intercession appears to you as the only thing in which your love can take refuge.

Blessings Dependent on Prayers

ANDREW MURRAY

Praying always with all prayer and supplication in the Spirit.
EPHESIANS 6:18

Will God really make the pouring out of blessing on others dependent on our prayers? Yes, He makes us His fellow workers. He has taken us into partnership in His work. If we fail to do our part, others will suffer and His work will suffer.

God has appointed intercession as one of the means by which others will be saved and Christians built up in the faith. People all over the world will receive life and blessing through our prayers. Should we not expect God's children to endeavor with all our strength to pray for God's blessing on the world?

Begin to use intercession as a means of grace for yourself and for others. Pray for your neighbors. Pray for sinners that they may come to Christ. Pray for your minister and for missionaries. Pray for your country and for government leaders. If you live a life completely for God, you will realize that the time spent in prayer is an offering pleasing to God.

Yes, "Praying always. . .with all perseverance and supplication for all saints." In so doing you will learn the lesson that intercession is the chief means of bringing others to Christ and bringing glory to God.

A Free Agent Enslaved

S. D. GORDON

Man *is* a free agent, so far as God is concerned. *And* he

179

is the most enslaved agent on the earth, so far as sin and selfishness and prejudice are concerned. The purpose of our praying is not to force or coerce his will; never that. It is to *free* his will of the warping influences that now twist it. It is to get the dust out of his eyes so his sight will be clear. And once he is free, able to see clearly, to balance things without prejudice, the whole probability is in favor of his using his will to choose the only right.

I want to suggest to you the ideal prayer for such a one. It is an adaptation of Jesus' own words. It may be pleaded with much variety of detail. It is this: deliver him from the evil one and work in him *Your will* for him, by Your power to Your glory, in Jesus' name. And there are three special passages upon which to base this prayer. The first is 1 Timothy 2:4, "[God] will have all men to be saved." That is God's will for your loved one. The second is 2 Peter 3:9, where it says that He is "not willing that any should perish, but that all should come to repentance." That is God's will, or desire, for the one you are thinking of now. The third passage is on our side who do the praying. It tells who may offer this prayer with assurance. John 15:7 says: "If ye abide in me, and my words abide in you, ye shall ask what ye will, and it shall be done unto you."

Saving the Life
S. D. Gordon

We cannot know a man's mental processes. It is surely true that if in the very last half-twinkling of an eye a person looks up toward God longingly, that look is the turning of the will to God. And that is quite enough. God is eagerly watching with hungry eyes for the quick

180

turn of a human eye up to Himself. Doubtless many a person has so turned in the last moment of his life when we were not conscious of his consciousness, nor aware of the movements of his outwardly unconscious subconsciousness. One may be unconscious of outer things and yet be keenly conscious toward God. . . .

Here is surely enough knowledge to comfort many a bereft heart, and enough, too, to make us pray persistently and believingly for loved ones because of prayer's incalculable power.

Giving God a Clear Road for Action
S. D. GORDON

There is a double side to the story I am about to tell: the side of the man who was changed and the side of the woman who prayed. He was almost a giant physically, keen mentally, a lawyer, and a natural leader. He had the conviction as a boy that if he became a Christian he was to preach. But he grew up a skeptic and read up and lectured on skeptical subjects. He was the representative of a district of his western home state in Congress, in his fourth term or so at this time.

The experience I am telling about came during a time that was not especially suited to meditation about God in the halls of Congress. Somehow he knew all the other skeptics who were in the lower house and they drifted together a good bit and strengthened each other by their talk.

One day as he was in his seat in the lower house, in the midst of the business of the hour, there came to him a conviction that God—the God in whom he did not believe—was right there above his head thinking about him and displeased at the way he was behaving toward Him. And he said to himself: "This is ridiculous. I've been working too hard; confined too closely; my mind is getting morbid. I'll go get some fresh air and shake myself."

And so he did. But the conviction only deepened and intensified. Day by day it grew. And that went on for weeks, into the fourth month as I recall his words. Then he planned to return home to attend to some business matters and to attend to some preliminaries for securing the nomination for the governorship of his state. And as I understand he was close to securing the nomination.

He reached his home and had hardly gotten there before he found that his wife and two others had entered into a holy compact of prayer for his conversion and had been so praying for some months. Instantly he thought of his unwelcome Washington experience and became intensely interested. But not wishing them to know of his interest, he asked carelessly when "this thing began." His wife told him the day. He did some quick mental figuring, and he said to me, "I knew almost instantly that the day she named fit into the calendar with the coming of that impression about God's presence."

He was greatly startled. He wanted to be thoroughly honest in all his thinking, and he said he knew that if a single fact of that sort could be established, of prayer producing such results, it carried the whole Christian scheme of belief with it. He did some stiff fighting within. Had he been wrong all those years? He sifted the matter back and forth as a lawyer would the evidence in a case. And he said to me, "As an honest man I was compelled to admit the facts, and I believe I might have been led to Christ that very night."

A few nights later he knelt at the altar in the Methodist meetinghouse in his hometown and surrendered his strong will to God. Then the early conviction of his boyhood days came back. He was to preach the gospel. And like Saul of old, he utterly changed his life and has been preaching the gospel with power ever since.

Then I was intensely fascinated in getting the other side, the praying side of the story. His wife had been a Christian for years, since before their marriage. But in some meetings in the home church she was led into a new, full surrender to Jesus Christ as Master, and had experienced a new consciousness of the Holy Spirit's presence and power. Almost at once came a new, intense desire for her husband's conversion. The compact of three was agreed upon, of daily prayer for him until the change came.

As she prayed that night after retiring to her room, she was in great distress of mind in thinking and praying for him. She could get no rest from this intense distress. At length she rose and knelt by the bedside to pray. As she was praying and distressed, an exquisitely quiet inner voice said, "Will you abide the consequences?" She was startled. Such a thing was wholly new to her. She did not know what it meant. And without paying any attention to it, she went on praying. Again came the same quietly spoken words to her ear, "Will you abide the consequences?" And again the half frightened feeling. She slipped back to bed to sleep, but sleep did not come. And back again to her knees, and again the patient, quiet voice.

This time with an earnestness bearing the impress

of her agony she said, "Lord, I will abide any consequence that may come if only my husband may be brought to You." And at once the distress slipped away, a sweet peace filled her being, and sleep quickly came. And while she prayed on for weeks and months patiently, persistently, day by day, the distress was gone, the sweet peace remained in the assurance that the result was surely coming. And so it was coming all those days down in the thick air of Washington's lower house, and so it did come.

What *was* the consequence to her? She had been a congressman's wife. She would likely have become the wife of the governor of her state, the first lady socially of the state. But she became a Methodist minister's wife, changing her home every few years. A very different position in many ways. No woman will be indifferent to the social difference involved. Yet rarely have I met a woman with more of that fine beauty that the peace of God brings, in her glad face and in her winsome smile.

Do you see the simple philosophy of that experience? Her surrender gave God a clear channel into that man's will. When the roadway was cleared, her prayer was a spirit-force traversing instantly the hundreds of intervening miles and affecting the spirit-atmosphere of his presence.

Shall we not put our wills fully in touch with God and persistently plead for each loved one, "Deliver him from the evil one, and work in him Your will, to Your glory, by Your power, in the Victor's name." And then add amen—so it *shall* be. Not so *may* it be—but so it *shall* be—an expression of confidence in Jesus' power.

A God Reminder
ANDREW MURRAY

Pray as one of God's reminders: "I have set watchmen upon thy walls...which shall never hold their peace day nor night: ye that make mention of the LORD, keep not silence" (Isaiah 62:6).

Study these words until your whole soul is filled with the realization: I am appointed as an intercessor. Enter God's presence with that faith. Approach the world's need with this thought: It is my job to intercede. Meditate on the fact that the Holy Spirit will teach you how to pray and what to pray for. Let it be a constant awareness: My great life work, like Christ's, is intercession. My purpose is to pray for believers and those who still do not know God.

Unceasing Intercession
ANDREW MURRAY

Pray without ceasing.
1 THESSALONIANS 5:17

The average Christian has a very different standard regarding a life of service to God than that which Scripture gives us. We think about our personal safety—grace to pardon our sin and to secure our entrance into heaven. The Bible's standard is that we surrender ourselves, our time, our thoughts, and our love to God.

To the average Christian the command "keep on praying" is a needless and impossible life of perfection. Who can do it? We can get to heaven without it.

However, to the true believer that command holds the promise of the highest happiness and of a life crowned by all the blessings that come through intercession. Through perseverance it becomes the highest aim and joy upon earth.

"Keep on praying." Take that word in faith as a promise of what God's Spirit will work in us. Let it become our heavenly calling. Christ said, "I in them and you in me." Let us believe that just as the Father worked in Him, Christ will work and pray in us. As the faith of our calling fills our hearts we literally will begin to feel there is nothing on earth to be compared with the privilege of walking without interruption in His holy presence, bringing others around us to the footstool of His throne, and receiving His power.

A Man for God's Plan
S. D. Gordon

The pathway from God to a human heart is through a human heart. When He came to the great strategic move in His plan, He Himself came down as a man and made that move. *He needs man for His plan.*

Faith in the Power of Prayer
Andrew Murray

I exhort therefore, that, first of all, supplications, prayers, intercessions, and giving of thanks, be made for all men; for kings, and for all that are in authority; that we may lead a quiet and peaceable life in all godliness and honesty.
1 Timothy 2:1–2

What a faith in the power of prayer! A few feeble and despised Christians are to influence the mighty Roman emperors and help in securing peace and quietness. Let us believe that prayer is a power that is taken up by God in His rule of the world. Let us pray for our country and its rulers; for all the rulers of the world; for rulers in cities or districts in which we are interested. When God's people unite in this, they may count upon their prayer effecting in the unseen world more than they know. Let faith hold this fast.

Scripture Index

Old Testament

Genesis
6:3...71
18:14...65, 93
18:30...41
19:29...41
22:15–18...43
32:24–30...85
32:26...41
32:28...41
45:5–8...59

Exodus
3:12...75
10:17...112
14:13...60
25:8...81
34:29...135

Joshua
7:11...77

Judges
15...114
15:19...114

1 Samuel
1:27...110

3:18...57
7:9...49
12:23...49, 78
15:11...49
15:22...71

1 Kings
17:24...111
18:1...172
18:37...105
18:43...161

1 Chronicles
4:10...110

2 Chronicles
20:2–5, 14–17, 20,
        22–23...72

Job
1:21...57
1:22...58
2:9–10...58
13:15...54

Psalms
5:3...126
19:8...56
20:1, 4...163

21:2...163
25:1...77
34:7...52
37:8...139
39:9...57
42:2...77
55:17...132
62:1...170
63:1...124
65:2...10
66:18...94
78:41...93
81:10...47
91:4...11
91:11–12...53
109:4...90
119:145...163
132:13...81
132:14...81
139:6...75
139:23–24...96

Ecclesiastes
5:2...90

Isaiah
27:5...161
53:12...171
55:6...39
56:7...72
59:2–3...94
62:6...62, 185
64:7...162

66:1–2...167

Jeremiah
29:13...155
32:17, 27...91, 93
33:3...92

Ezekiel...
36:37...92

Daniel
6:10...127
10...100

Micah
7:7...93

Malachi
3:10...44

New Testament

Matthew
5:8...54
6:6...133, 134, 135
6:8...83, 84
6:25...55
7:7–8...134
8:5–13...36
8:8, 10...36
9:29...68
10:29–31...52

11:28...165
13:58...34, 93
15:27–28...168
15:28...36
17:14–21...102
17:19–20...140
17:20–21...138
17:21...140
21:22...50
23:37...11
26:39...108
26:40...121
28:18, 20...75

Mark
6:5–6...34
9:17–29...102
9:23...43, 111
9:24...43
11:24...36, 40, 42, 74

Luke
2:47...27
6:12...121
9:18...130
11:5–8...62
11:7...38, 178
11:9–10...134
11:11, 13...150
11:13...135
12:6...54
18:1–8...101
18:41...88, 158

21:36...69
22:32...15
22:42...147
23:34...15
24:30–31...79
24:49...45

John
6:15...130
11:41–42...34, 111
13–17...24
13:7...54
14:1...162
14:11–12...162
14:13–14...24
14:13...103
14:14...103
14:19–20...123
14:21...78
15:5...124
15:7...63, 103, 104, 180
15:7, 10...166
15:7, 16...24
15:16...19, 63
16:14...26
16:23...24
16:23–24...105
16:23–24, 26...24
17:11, 15...87
20:16...78
20:28...163
21:7...54

Acts
1:14...46
2:4...46
6:4...90
9:36–43...113
12...66, 113
12:12...66
28...113

Romans
8:26...45
8:27...16
8:28...58
8:32...83
8:38–39...53
12:1...71

1 Corinthians
7:32...139
9:9...54
13:4–5...23
14:15...164

2 Corinthians
1:11...43
3:5...171
4:17...59
6:16...176
12:9...171

Galatians
4:6...150
5:24...139

Ephesians
1:16–19...64
1:17–20...61
1:18–19...8
3:14...124
3:16...123, 150
3:16–17...61
3:20...50
3:20–21...61
6:10...61
6:11–18...99
6:18...179

Philippians
4:4–5...148
4:6...29, 86, 87, 148, 149,
        153, 157
4:6–7...137
4:7...87

Colossians
1:29...80
4:2–3...38

1 Thessalonians
5:16–18...73, 149
5:17...108, 185
5:18...73

1 Timothy
2:1...164
2:1–2...186
2:4...180

2 Timothy
1:6...162

Hebrews
4:12...89, 145
4:14, 16...172
7:25...14
10:36...147
10:37...115
11:32–35...110

James
4:2...95
4:3...95, 104
4:6...169
4:8...80
5...68
5:11...58
5:13–18...30
5:16...63, 169, 172

1 Peter
4:7–8...22
5:7...139

2 Peter
1:4...42
3:9...180

1 John
1:9...10
3:21–22...88
5:14...142, 145

5:16...88

Revelation
3:19...146
8:1, 3...128
8:3–5...76
22:9...76